1979

To Pam

Sept - 1979
With love from
Mum - Dad
x x

To Pam

Sept - 1979

Janet Marsh's
NATURE
DIARY

Scabious
Wild Carrot.
Sept. 78

Janet Marsh's
NATURE DIARY

Text and Illustrations

by

JANET MARSH

MICHAEL JOSEPH

LONDON

First published in Great Britain by Michael Joseph Ltd
44 Bedford Square, London WC1 1979

ISBN 0 7181 1796 4

Set by The Curwen Press, London. Printed and bound in
Italy by Arnoldo Mondadori, Verona

Insects amongst common wild thyme, July 78.

*To my parents
and Anthony*

INTRODUCTION

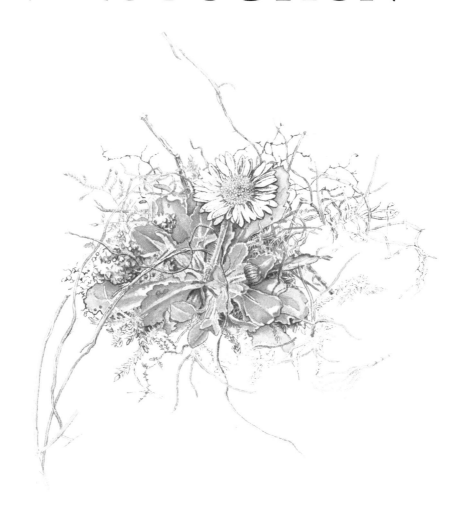

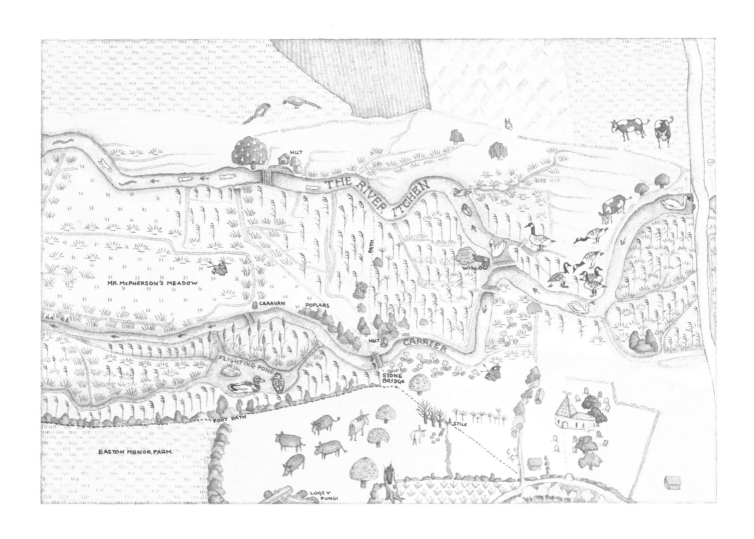

THE RIVER ITCHEN

MR. McPHERSON'S MEADOW

HUT

PATH

WILLOW

CARRIER

CARAVAN

POPLARS

HUT

FLIGHTING POND

STONE BRIDGE

STILE

FOOT PATH

EASTON MANOR FARM.

LOGS Y FUNGI

	Agricultural land.		Marsh		Small bullocks.	Canadian geese.
	Wetlands.		Grazing land.		Large cows.	Best areas to observe butterflies.
	Reed beds.		Sweet chestnut tree		Hollow willow.	Best area for marsh marigolds.
	Bulrush		Hawthorn		Hogweed.	Wild garlic.
	Tussocks.		Wych elms.		Ink caps.	Railway sleeper bridge.

INTRODUCTION

The River Itchen rises near the village of Cheriton, Hampshire, and is about thirty miles long. The Upper Itchen extends to the ancient cathedral town of Winchester, a distance of four miles; and it is the Upper Itchen Valley, with its varied and abundant species of plant, animal and insect life, that has held me spellbound for some twelve years.

The valley is a microcosm of all that is most precious and delightful about the English countryside; I have been studying in this diary probably the last, unstocked, chalk stream in Western Europe. Owing to the wide variety of habitats, ranging from chalk downland, improved and unimproved grassland, herb with meadow and fen, sub-aquatic and aquatic, there are innumerable species of insects, plants and birds. The valley is the most important migration route in England for moths travelling northwards. But tragically, this valley is threatened by an extension of the M3 motorway. Such a motorway crossing the valley would have far-reaching and disastrous effects. I believe that the present by-pass should be improved and a unique environment preserved.

On the left bank of the Upper Itchen, the village of Easton runs like a ribbon along narrow country roads. It was here that I first saw the water meadows and the wide river itself. I was fourteen at the time and on a school exeat. My mother and I walked across a field in driving rain and squelched through extensive bog to the relative shelter of an old green caravan. My father was in his element; he had found the perfect chalk stream at last. Crawling around in deep camouflage, he settled down to a serious, wet, but enjoyable bout of fishing. I peered through the cobwebbed glass of the caravan, huddling near to the candle, our only source of light and heat, for my first glimpse, a rather miserable one, of the Itchen Valley.

At first we had nowhere to stay but the pub, then when a puppy joined the family my father bought and renovated a tiny ancient cottage in the heart of the village.

Easton village is small, predominantly thatched, with the most beautiful church situated near the river. The people, and especially their gardens, are very different from the Sussex village in which I was brought up. There is one particularly striking garden, on the way to the Chestnut Horse pub, surrounded by a lavender hedge, bursting with colour, flowers growing in and around arches of sweet pea canes. The gardens vary from simple allotments to large formal designs, but the cottage garden and vegetable patch abound. Throughout the village, in every nook and cranny of the old

stone walls, creeps ivy-leaved toadflax intertwined with aubretia, mosses, lichens and ferns. Our own small, relatively new garden is beginning to take shape with its great rounded bushes of Old English roses, buddleia, and a vegetable garden and nettle patch for caterpillars and butterflies.

At the top of the rolling chalk hills near Easton are ancient hedgerows, with a track running between them. They are an endless source of fascination. In the autumn there is nothing to beat their beauty; old man's beard winds itself around wild rose bushes and to the very tops of the trees, carving intricate patterns with its thick, woody stems. White and black bryony glisten; black privet berries, sloes, snowberries, wild plums, beautiful spindle berries and many others dazzle the eyes and the imagination. These hedgerows, which are part of our natural heritage, are under constant threat and many have now been destroyed.

The surrounding land is devoted to crops; small, sturdy cattle graze by the river. Extensive areas of the river's flood plain were converted to water meadows in the first half of the nineteenth century; before that the Upper Itchen was considered unsuitable for watering because of underlying peat. The water meadows were essentially a permanent and often elaborate irrigation system, formed into successive ridges and furrows. Water was led into 'carriers' along the crowns of the ridges and permitted to overflow down their sides to the drawns (drains) which carried the water to the main river and off the meadow.

Water meadows were laborious to build and laborious to maintain, and watering required accuracy of timing for maximum benefit. The meadows were generally flooded in February to provide March grass for ewes and lambs. Grass is stimulated into new growth because the stream water in winter is warmer than the surrounding land. Flooding assisted both the July hay crop and grazing in the autumn.

With the loss of men knowledgeable in water-meadow management, known as 'drowners' or 'floaters', and the ever increasing cost of labour, the aqueducts and sluices fell into disuse.

However, the effects of the system, with its many sluices, underground waterways, bridges, drains, channels and, not least, the carrier, remain to dominate the landscape. Indeed, many of the sluices are still in use, and the ridges and bridges in the extensive reed beds between river and carrier are very useful when the water-table level is high.

Reeds.

The ridge and furrow systems can be seen at any time of the year, but are most distinctive in the summer. The lush plant life growing in the ditches, such as the marsh marigolds and yellow flag irises, mark them out as intricate, green-blue and yellow ribbons running across the valley. A number of the ditches are permanently flooded, making excellent nesting areas for the many water birds. Other ditches flood in times of heavy rain. In general, the wetter the site and the more peaty the soil, the richer the land is in plant and insect life. Intense grazing favours the grasses, but at the expense of flowering plants. In small grazed areas, tall herbs, rushes and reeds invade at the expense of smaller, less vigorous plants. In my area of study, large areas of the water meadows have been fenced off from the cattle, forming extensive reed beds and carr; and the remaining meadows, although grazed, seem to have reached a botanically happy medium. The site is particularly rich in marsh orchids, marsh marigolds, yellow flag irises, skullcap and meadowsweet; the list is endless; the flowers in the meadows at the height of summer have to be seen to be believed.

The most exciting visual experiences of my life have been gained whilst sitting still in the meadow near the old green caravan. More is to be learned by

[12]

quietly watching and listening to bird, insect or animal for a few hours than anything the text book can offer. Flowers and grasses stretch above one's head, whilst spiders and brightly-coloured beetles wend their way between the stems. Different species of striped hoverflies, bees and insects of every shape, size and colour variation, investigate the flowers for pollen. After a few hours a pattern emerges; every creature has a territory; the butterflies, which often return to the same plant within a very short space of time, are the most obvious example.

Lying on the ground when quaking grass covers the valley is an unforgettable experience, for as far as the eye can see the valley shimmers with a shining film of mauve.

Looking at a male brimstone butterfly feeding, with the sun directly behind it, is a marvellous, if fleeting experience. The yellow-green wings become translucent, showing the delicate pattern of veins and the arched body of the insect. The meadows transport me to another, quite separate world.

Extensive colonies of reeds, up to eight feet in height, grow where the meadow has been fenced off. Enormous tussocks mark the man-made ditches on either side of the path running from the carrier to the main river. A few hawthorns, alders and small willows grow in amongst the reeds; the latter were planted to serve as a wind break. The reeds themselves are majestic, sometimes dark brown after the rain and sometimes pale and stark, with pale spikelets in the wintry sun. It is in August, when their foliage is a lush green and their 'plumes' purple-tinted, that they are at their most attractive.

Bulrushes, or reedmace, grow by the entrance to the flighting ponds, at the crossroads between the Upper Itchen and the carrier. They stand like soldiers, rigid and erect, their dark flower spikes contrasting with the pale reeds in winter. Intermingled with the reedmace and reeds are bur reed, great willow herb, yellow loosestrife and other water-loving, vigorous plants and grasses.

[13]

The fens teem with bird life: sedge warblers, reed buntings, reed warblers, and, on rare occasions, water-rails are seen. In the narrow waterways and the flighting pond, on the left of the carrier, there are coot, little grebe, tufted duck, grey wagtails, mallard, teal and a pair of kingfishers. Lapwings, snipe, redshanks and wagtails are common in the meadows.

The Upper Itchen itself flows in a wide, shallow bed between ill-defined margins marked by sedge tussocks and an enormous variety of bankside vegetation. A small, well-kept path winds its way along the river, the tall plants acting as a screen between fisherman and fish. Purple loosestrife, hemp agrimony, common comfrey, creeping jenny, rosebay willowherb, water avens, orange balsam, the giant water dock and many others make up the riparian vegetation. I have also found two plants of dark mullein, which is quite rare.

In the shallows near the bank, water speedwells, forget-me-nots and brookline grow amongst beds of shining green watercress. Water crowfoot, an underwater plant, carpets the river with its white and yellow floating flowers during May and June.

The river is spring-fed and therefore water temperatures remain relatively constant throughout the year. The systems are thus stable and rich in nutrients, and the fertility of both plants and animals is high. The river bed is covered with various species of water weed unless it has been recently cut. Water crowfoot, fool's watercress and water parsnip flourish where the current is fast, as they have strong rooting systems. Canadian pondweed and starwort dominate areas where the current has become sluggish and silt has built up.

Periodic weed cutting by the water-keepers reduces the weed cover, and silt is washed downstream; but this in turn provides the trout with territories and spawning grounds. The 'coarse' fish are discouraged as most spawn in the weed.

The invertebrate fauna of the river can be seen mainly in larval form when taking jam-jar samples from the river bed. Caddis fly larvae in their different and colourful protective cases are very common, as are the may fly, stone fly, alder fly and black fly nymphs. Amongst the weed it is easy to scoop up water lice, shrimps, tiny leeches, beetles, water spiders, various worms and snails of many different shapes and sizes. I still swim in the crystal-clear water in the summer despite them all!

The three British aquatic mammals, water vole, water shrew and otter are all present in my small area. Water voles and shrews are very common, especially the former which make lattice work out of the banks wherever possible. Towards the end of my diary the otter's home is identified; I must have been within feet of the breeding holt without realising it. It is now very rare due to disturbance, pollution, but mainly destruction of habitat. There is an established breeding population in the Upper Itchen Valley. As the bankside vegetation diminishes downstream, so too does the otter, for both breeding holt and daytime hover in or near river banks must be protected by vegetation in a secluded spot. The otter's haven is the large meadow on the right of the old green

[15]

caravan. But how long will it remain his haven?

It is through this meadow, which once supported large populations of locally distributed plants – now limited in distribution because there is so little suitable habitat remaining – that the six-lane motorway will pass, over the river and carrier. The flighting pond will be drained, many drainage systems will be diverted and the peat layers stripped in order to sink thirty-feet concrete pylons into the valley beds. According to a recent government survey, this area was declared to be of Grade One ecological value.

The Itchen Valley, with its unique bankside vegetation and profuse animal life, must be left intact, for it is part of our natural heritage. I hope my paintings will give the reader some idea of the beauty and endless fascination of the valley, for which this book is an urgent plea for conservation.

Daisy. Dec. 15th 78.

THE DIARY

JANUARY

January 6th

I walked into the cottage at Easton and at once noticed a hibernating, small tortoise-shell butterfly near the back door. I immediately got on to the floor with my pencil, paper, paints and brushes just in case the central heating coming on would disturb it and it should awaken and disappear. What an effort it is painting on the floor, but a perfect butterfly and one unlikely to move is such a bonus.

The aquarium had gone through yet another stage. At first I had been worried about the increase in the shrimp population; for in their very weight and size they had seemed to dominate totally. But now the snails too had increased in size and multiplied and there were only six or seven shrimps left. A predator, or predators had been solving the shrimp problem.

Whilst I was watching two caddis fly larvae intently, I became aware that two creatures resembling sticks had shot out from beneath a couple of rocks. One was larger than the other, both were pink-blue in colour and both kept absolutely still, like ramrods, until a shrimp was near enough to lunge at. I have only seen a few attempts at shrimp-gathering and they were unsuccessful; however, their reactions were a hundred per cent better than those of the particular species of caddis fly larvae that we have in the aquarium.

The day was cold and the winter sun shone weakly as I walked down to the river. On the southern bank, well sheltered by hedgerows, I saw a lovely celandine in flower, and further on, near the church, a dandelion and a wild geranium.

I opened the gate to the children's playing field. Tiny nettles, already green, grew in an ominous way on either side of the path. I stood on the stile at the end of the field, affording myself the maximum view possible of the carrier and the main river. I looked for the Canada geese and saw

[19]

shrimps.

Underside of snail.

Fleshy vulnerable body.

Caddis cases are always open at both ends, in this case the rear opening is very narrow. Movements of larva's body draws water through the case, in this way the caddis gets a constant supply of oxygen which is extracted from the water through gills along its body.

Rudmace.

them, as usual, intently cropping the grass in the distance, on the right
bank of the main river. One hybrid goose, half Canada and half domestic,
stood large and white, surveying the scene with two of his henchmen.

The donkey seemed particularly keen to greet me, and with quite
swift steps came to meet me as I walked through the grazing field to the
carrier. Having had a few rather unfortunate experiences with this
donkey, I made my way briskly towards the nearest stretch of barbed
wire and slipped under it, with a sense of relief. A large brown trout saw
me and, with a few deft movements of its tail, was out of sight in a clump
of weed, leaving a bow wave behind it. This is the time of year that trout
lay their eggs in 'redds' – hollows which they make by the movements of
their bodies in the coarse gravel parts of the river bed. The female makes
the hollow and lies in it as she lays her eggs, which are fertilised by the
male, externally, as he lies alongside her.

A water vole plopped into the river beside me and I saw the silver
air-bubbles trapped in its coat as it darted by. Then, hearing a chatter of
birds above me, I looked up and was thrilled to see about twenty long-
tailed tits silhouetted against the sky.

The bulrushes were almost ready to unfurl and shed their thousands of
seeds. They stood dark against the pale whispering reeds that surrounded
them.

January 10th
Bitterly cold weather but clear skies. I went down to the river with my
tuning-fork and a small box; and I tried as best I could to mimic the
correct vibrations of a fly trapped in a web amidst the ivy-clad branches,
but not a sign of a spider.

After about half an hour I moved on to investigate new pastures.
My footsteps crunched amongst the frosted leaves which sparkled in the
light. I went to the water meadow between the carrier and the main
river, where the damage from the winds was tremendous. As I was
using the tuning-fork busily amongst the fallen trees, I caught sight of
Mr Fox, the water-keeper. Before he was able to make some witty
remark about there being no pianos around, I asked him about the

Canada geese, as I had spent much time in trying to get close enough to draw them, but without success. "Get up at first light and walk towards them with your back to the sun and you will be able to walk right up to them," he said. I ruled that out – I would probably be as sleepy as the geese – and in this weather it is difficult enough to draw anyway.

January 11th
Today I went off to look for mistletoe. I had asked Mr Fox and he had told me of its whereabouts. It was in a farmer's private land behind Curry's training centre, the big white house on the hill which I had often seen from the river. I got out of the car and passed some workmen having tea in their van. Half an hour later, having jumped and scrambled and prodded with long sticks, I emerged triumphant, with a piece of mistletoe I'd found growing on a lime tree. The workmen were still there and made, as I had feared, some interesting comments about my find. It was indeed a little late for Christmas festivities!

When home, I studied my hard-earned specimen; it looked almost plastic in texture, the ripe berries were white, while the others were a yellow-green. I had somehow expected more than this plant had to offer, and I never did paint it.

Instead, I went down to the river to gather some more excitements for the tiny aquarium. Well wrapped up, and equipped with jam jars and green plastic sieve, I investigated the river. The crowd of workmen on the road looked fascinated and were laughing, but I ignored the merriment and tried to look as aloof as one can, standing in the river with a sieve. Having collected some weed, caddis larvae and freshwater shrimps, I wandered nonchalantly towards the gate and road. And I listened, with a rather embarrassed smile on my face to such remarks as, "How many fish did you catch?" and others.

January 15th
The day before yesterday the whole of Britain was hit by the worst storms since 1953. Eighty-mile-an-hour winds swept the country and the Thames came within two feet of flooding. I walked down to the river, not

Earwigs.

– Caddis larva-like
creatures.

Emerald green turf found
by the river.

only to look for empty caddis larvae cases, but also to see the extent of the damage. The ivy, which was thick and heavy on many trees, had caused eight to fall in the high winds along the edge of Mr Brown's fields. No doubt they would be removed fairly soon. I searched for spiders in the ivy, for they are said to lie in wait there for hibernating butterflies, and other insects which shelter in the bright green leaves. However, I had forgotten to bring down the tuning-fork, which was bought especially for spider-catching, and had no luck whatsoever; but I think this was largely because it was so bitterly cold and my hands were numb.

Walked along the river and found some beautiful emerald-green turf, a stunning sight at this time of year. The cattle drink was frozen, and so was I after about an hour wading in the carrier with wellingtons on and an old sieve in hand. Eventually, with my hands bright red from the icy water, I retreated, having found only three kinds of caddis larvae cases, due to the bad light. I had filled a jam jar full of shrimps and nymphs for our small aquarium and, clutching the string, I walked rather briskly back to the cottage. To my delight, I had also brought up a tiny red water-spider on my hand. The underside is bright red, and on its back it has a gold streak. The whole insect is smaller than a pin head.

Spider upside down.

Beautiful shapes and colours of riverside vegetation during early February.

FEBRUARY

great
spotted
woodpecker.

February 3rd

I went along the road to Winchester that crosses the Itchen, as far as the bridge. I collected some dried reeds and saw that young growth had started in the areas that had been covered by flood water. I walked along the main river to the sharp bend where the carrier flows from it, crossed the bridge and followed the right bank of the lesser river. I had never seen the river so full or so cloudy; for the first time I could not see the bottom.

One bulrush stood alone amongst the reeds. Its head was looking untidy, as the seeds were coming away and had already gone from one strip about an inch wide down one side of it. The rich dark-brown velvetiness was beginning to look pitted.

I heard a long, repeated "tchnik, tchnik" as I walked through the children's playing field towards the river. I saw the woodpeckers; a greater spotted one was feeding on the already dead branches of the dying wych elms. These beautiful tall trees, growing in a line on a bank in the meadow, are dying of Dutch elm disease. Some have already been cut down.

It started to pour with rain as I reached the fishing hut by the brick bridge, so I sheltered and watched the poor old donkey cowering in the lee of the field hedge. But the sun soon came out, creating a most beautiful steep rainbow, with very broad and pronounced colours.
A long way off I saw the other end of it, only a small piece of rainbow; the sky in between being clear and blue.

It became a lovely afternoon, the sun shining towards me as I walked by the water, high-lighting the feathers of a pair of swans: their wings rose like white sails at the sight of the dog.

I walked along the full, fast-flowing carrier until I came to the little

[26]

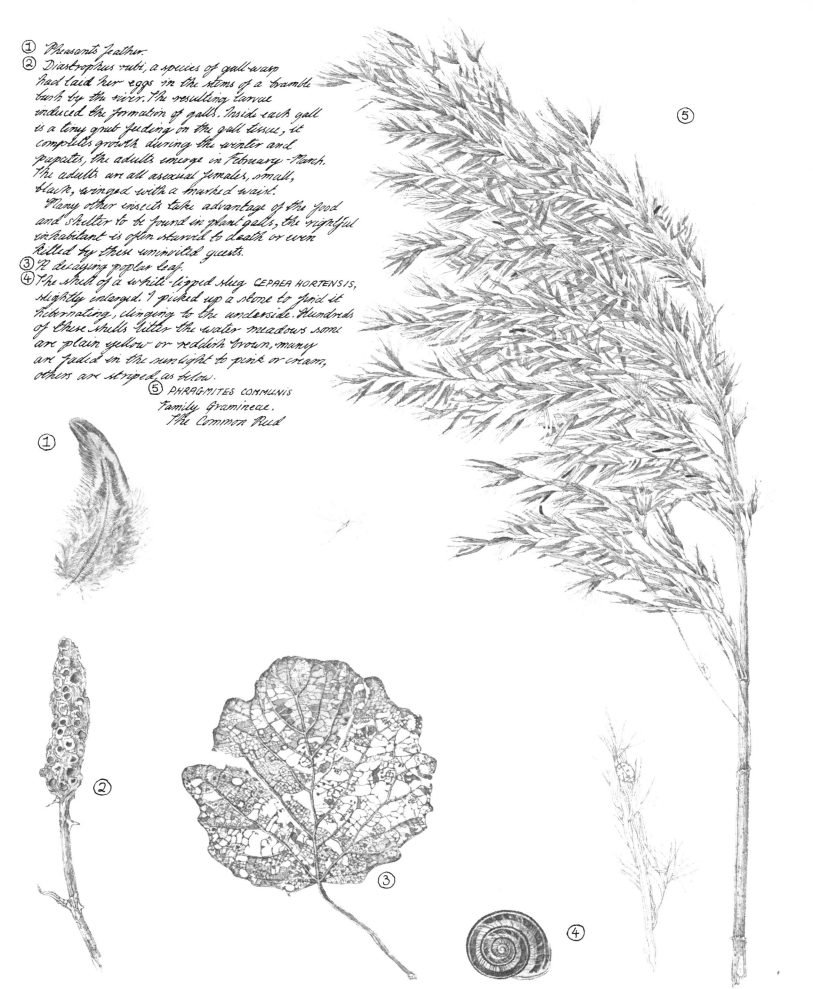

① Pheasants feather.
② Diastrophus rubi, a species of gall-wasp
had laid her eggs in the stems of a bramble
bush by the river. The resulting larvae
induced the formation of galls. Inside each gall
is a tiny grub feeding on the gall tissue, it
completes growth during the winter and
pupates, the adults emerge in February-March.
The adults are all asexual females, small,
black, winged with a marked waist.
   Many other insects take advantage of the food
and shelter to be found in plant galls, the rightful
inhabitant is often starved to death or even
killed by these uninvited guests.
③ A decaying poplar leaf.
④ The shell of a white-lipped slug CEPAEA HORTENSIS,
slightly enlarged. I picked up a stone to find it
hibernating, clinging to the underside. Hundreds
of these shells litter the water meadows some
are plain yellow or reddish brown, many
are faded in the sunlight to pink or cream,
others are striped as below.
          ⑤ PHRAGMITES COMMUNIS
             Family Gramineae.
             The Common Reed

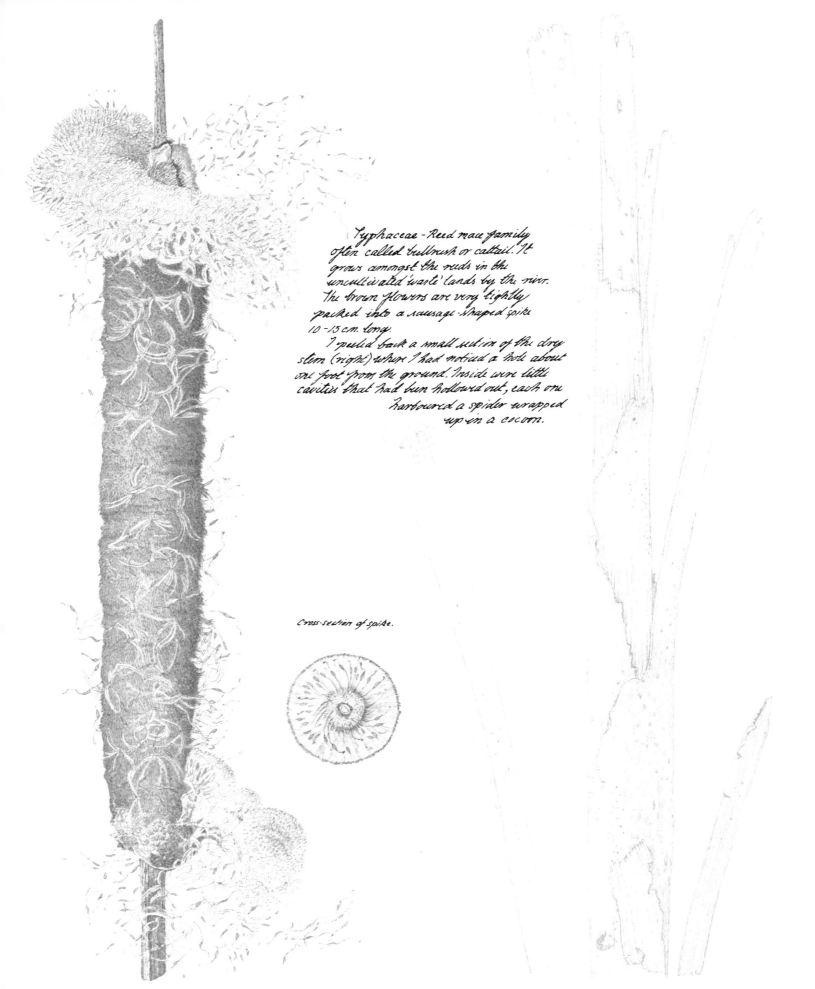

Typhaceae - Reed mace family
often called bullrush or cattail. It
grows amongst the reeds in the
uncultivated 'waste' lands by the river.
The brown flowers are very tightly
packed into a sausage-shaped spike
10-15 cm. long.
    I peeled back a small section of the dry
stem (right) where I had noticed a hole about
one foot from the ground. Inside were little
cavities that had been hollowed out, each one
        harboured a spider wrapped
            up in a cocoon.

Cross-section of spike.

wooden bridge by the pumping station. I noticed that the new growth of the yellow flag iris had been cropped down by the horses grazing here now, while the new growth of the reeds along the river bank had been eaten by the water voles, for the horses cannot reach them.

The sun was low as I turned at the bridge and looked over the water meadows. They shone with winter colours, the distant bare trees, the greeny-grey of the poplars, the warm rich colour of alders and a mingling of many tones and shades of brown. The willow twigs are beginning to get their glowing, golden look.

Whilst walking amongst the reeds bed where the carrier flows from the main river, I saw the entrance to a short-tailed vole's underground burrow. One spring I saw its ball-shaped nest, beautifully made out of woven grass, hanging out over the water, probably to protect it from predators.

February 5th

Some birds seem to be pairing. I had taken my parents' dog, Fred, an outsize 'standard' poodle, with me and he put up a pair of partridge in the meadow by the main river, and a pair of mallard flew overhead. The many duck that live among the reeds by the smaller carrier seemed to be absent; there is a very large gathering of mallard on Arlesford lake; perhaps they have gone there.

A flock of about twenty lapwings flew over. There seem to be many more of these birds now than there were a few years ago.

Four young mute swans were on the carrier, two males (cobs), and two females (pens). Their plumage, still immature, was of a mottled, soft brown colour. Some new primary feathers were white but their beaks were still pale.

There are long lines of newly-dug mole-hills near the river's edge, many of them flecked white with small pieces of chalk. Moles do not seem to mind sodden ground, and I hear from Mr Fox that they are excellent swimmers when there is flooding.

One fish rose to a large dark olive fly. A few spinners were flying over the river bank.

[29]

The osiers are now showing their fire-like colours, standing out dramatically against the bare branches of other trees, as are the yews and ivy. The beds of norfolk reeds are a beautiful sight, their stems arching in unison before the wind, with plumes like feathered fingers.

February 25th
It has rained hard today. The snowdrops along the hedgerows looked drenched and bedraggled as I, looking much the same way as them, made my way towards the river at a quick trot.

On the way to the gate where the snowdrops grow, I met a small boy with a wheelbarrow, going in the opposite direction. He stared with disbelief at the extraordinary sight which greeted him: a girl wearing a silver raincoat (the kind fashionable in London a few years ago), a purple and yellow hand-knitted scarf, and an outsize pair of green wellingtons with socks protruding.

On this occasion I was searching for fungi and lichens, plenty to be found by the river, but more to be found in the churchyard. Feeling furtive, with a small knife in my pocket, I approached that hallowed ground rather regretting my conspicuous outfit. The rain drizzled on and I felt sure that even a dedicated churchgoer would not be out in this sort of weather. I was proved wrong and I retreated hastily to look at the old brick walls along the way. I passed the snowdrops and walked on into the field, making a bee-line for the line of elms. I could not understand why the bark hadn't been burnt from those that had been cut down, to try and stop the Dutch elm disease from spreading; but as I wanted to paint the bark, it was useful to me that it had been left.

Half-way across the stile I noticed, with some foreboding, that there · were now four large horses in the field which runs down to the carrier.

Mountains of chopped trees still lay untouched on the grass. I clambered on to the trunks, most of which are now bare, as the bark has fallen to the ground. The outer bark is pitted with large worm-like holes, intermingled with lichens and fungi. The inner bark is fascinating and beautiful, in a sinister sort of way. Large and small elm bark larvae have hollowed out a worm-like shape in the centre of the bark, fanning

Mosses and lichens are abundant by the river, many of the mosses grow in the long, cool ditch running parallel to the right bank and the majority of the lichens covering the ivy on the overhanging poplar trees. The ivy is still living but it is almost hidden with a beautiful and intricate carpet of many different species of lichen.

The best collection of mosses and lichens however belongs to the church yard. The ancient grave stones are encrusted with orange-red, pale green and blue-grey lichens and covered with dark green Bryum argenteum which clings closely to the stone making a fern-like shape. It is a particularly attractive moss with a silver sheen, the dark green often turning into a rich rust.

On the wooden bridges, the windowsill of the hut and on grave-stones, branches and garden walls, I found the beautiful deep yellow and orange lichen Xanthoria Parietina, as illustrated on Plate 6.

① BRACHYTHECIUM VELUTINUM. (moss).
② PARMELIA SULCATA (leafy sp. lichen).
③ ACROCLADIUM CUSPIDATUM (moss).
④ EVERINA PRUNASTRI (strap-shaped lichen).

This robust moss thrives in the damp ditch, harbouring many little creatures and innumerable spiders. I have seen the moss simply covered with gossamer webs of different shapes and sizes.

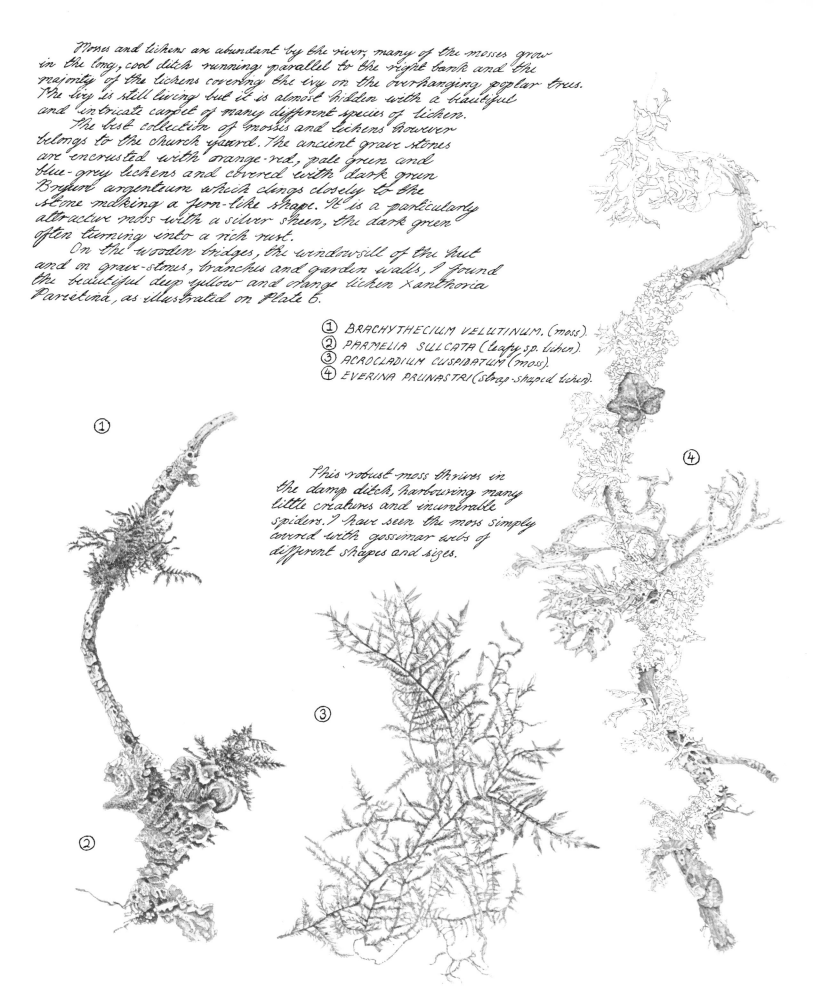

outwards in every direction to form a pattern. Some river-like shapes run deep and are thick; on other pieces of bark the pattern is very fine and thread-like. Last year I took large sections of the bark to my flat in London, because of its exquisite 'engravings'. This same bark has now crumbled and next year will be unrecognisable.

My wellington boots slid on the slimy surface of the trunks; some of the various species of fungi were rotting underfoot and new fungi were appearing in their place.

In December, I had seen some rather spectacular fungus appearing on the bark. It was orange and rounded and grew in a clump, and on every fungus was a big bright orange droplet which sparkled in the pale winter light. There was no trace of it now, but many exciting varieties had taken its place. Beside my left foot, an enormous fungus was growing; orange and now decaying, its diameter was about nine inches. On the under surface of the wood grew white rounds of flat fungi, reminding me of the rounds of yellow lichen on the grave stones. There were dots of orange on the trunks where there had been little decay, alongside cup-shaped, rubbery, almost transparent fungi. Soft bracket-like fungus grew everywhere, with a green-white and brown upper surface; it looked almost hairy, and had an orange, smooth, rubbery underside. A bright orange, mushroom-like fungus grew in clumps in various stages of maturity. I carefully took a sample of each to study and, on turning, discovered that I was being watched by Beppo, the donkey, who could be vicious if one had no sandwiches. I turned out my pockets for him, indicating that I had no food. Eventually, putting back his ears in disgust, he went away. Clambering down with my booty, I headed for the stile as the rain was getting uncomfortably heavy.

Two of the largest horses trotted up to investigate me. Horses frighten me, especially in twos and threes. Like many other children in my village, I had been taken to riding school when very young – a good experience according to my parents. I won prizes for jumping and they must have thought that I was doing well, until one day I told them that it was only sheer fear that had kept me in the saddle, desperately clinging to the mane. I looked at the horses, and they looked back and rolled their eyes

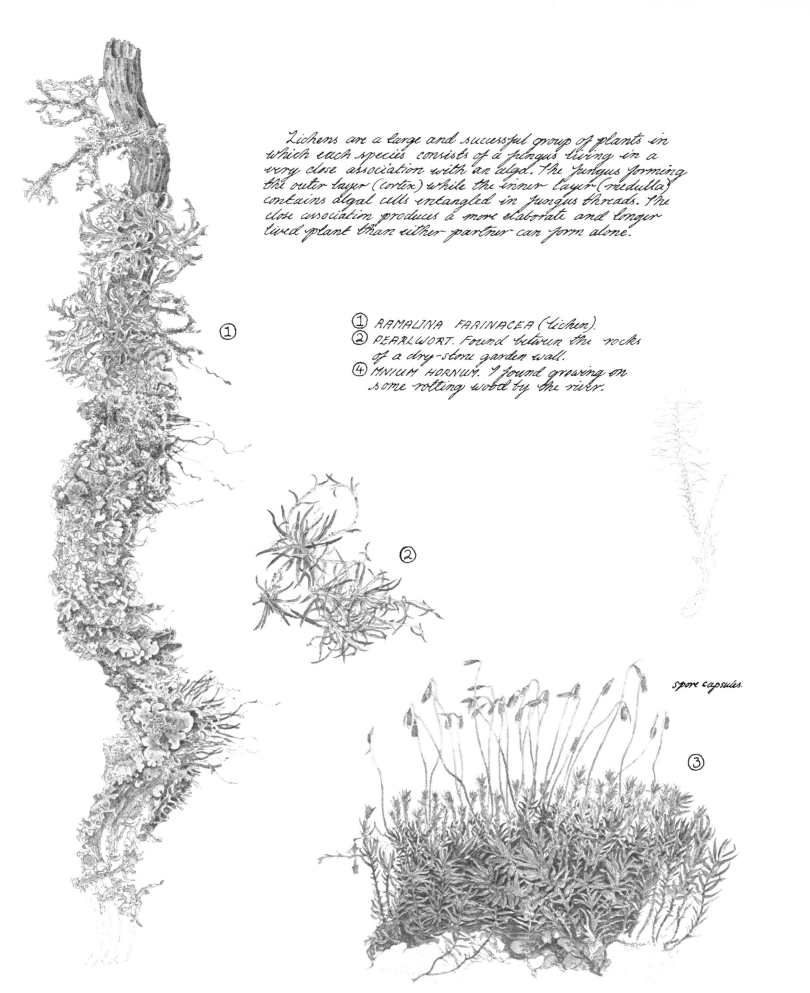

Lichens are a large and successful group of plants in which each species consists of a fungus living in a very close association with an alga. The fungus forming the outer layer (cortex) while the inner layer (medulla) contains algal cells entangled in fungus threads. The close association produces a more elaborate and longer lived plant than either partner can form alone.

① RAMALINA FARINACEA (lichen).
② PEARLWORT. Found between the rocks of a dry-stone garden wall.
④ MNIUM HORNUM. I found growing on some rotting wood by the river.

spore capsules.

Just a few of the lichens, mosses and fungi all to be found within a small area of the Upper Itchen valley.

A tiny clump of moss and lichen I found between two railway sleepers on the bridge. Note the beautiful, red, spore producing apothecia. March.

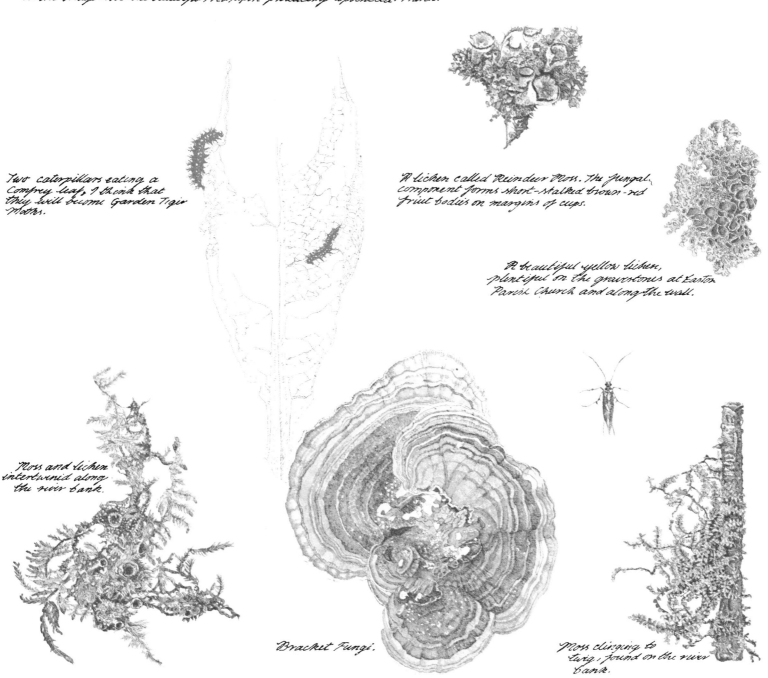

Two caterpillars eating a Comfrey leaf, I think that they will become Garden Tiger Moths.

A lichen called Reindeer Moss. The fungal component forms short-stalked brown-red fruit bodies on margins of cups.

A beautiful yellow lichen, plentiful on the gravestones at Easton Parish Church and along the wall.

Moss and lichen intertwined along the river bank.

Bracket Fungi.

Moss clinging to twig, found on the river bank.

Small clump of orange fungi growing
on the trunk of a dead elm.

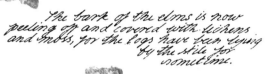

The bark of the elms is now
peeling off and covered with lichens
and moss, for the logs have been lying
by the stile for
sometime.

Very like the 'Ear Fungus' which grows on elder, this specimen
was also growing on the elm logs. The inner surface is shiny,
the outer velvety, it is a jelly-like, slightly translucent fungus.

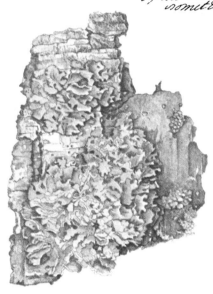

An attractive pink-brown lichen.

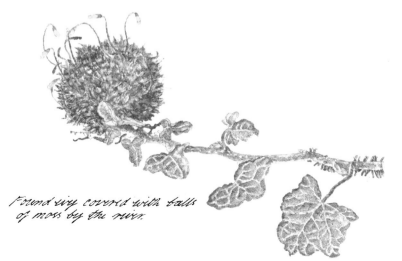

Found ivy covered with balls
of moss by the river.

Moss, showing ripe capsules.

Grey Squirrel

Hind legs.

in a worrying way. I stood on the nearest log to look tall and then flapped my silver mac at them. It worked; they were gone and I was doing the hundred yards to the stile.

Once over, I relaxed and looked around me, hoping to gain a vague impression of the colours of late February. I was now sick of what seemed like never-ending winter; I have almost forgotten what a green leaf looks like, or the carpet of subtle greens that clad the trees during early spring. The reeds, some upright and some flattened by wind and rain, are a soft white rust and I admit that they do look beautiful, even through a curtain of rain. Hundreds of mole-hills surrounding the river, which was almost in flood, looked virtually black against the pale flow of the water. The rain trickled down my neck and I started back, making a mental note to paint a tiny landscape, however small, before all the colours changed again.

In fact I started to draw a squirrel, which had fallen foul of my father-in-law's shotgun! This pretty, grey-brown, rat-like creature had tempted providence and dug up all the crocus bulbs. I had been there at the kill and, although I'd been sorry and reproachful, it proved to be an ideal opportunity for getting to know the shape and colour of the animal.

MARCH

March 3rd

The first glimpse of the sun for at least eight days. Paint brushes lie untouched as Anthony and I prepare to go down to the river.

It feels and sounds like the beginning of spring. The parrot cocked an eye at the starlings on the uppermost branches of the old yew tree. They shook the last of the raindrops off their feathers with vigorous movements of shiny wing and tail feathers.

With my faded green hat to protect my eyes, a few small plastic bags in which to collect things of interest, and my camera, I set off.

The cabbage field as usual was a great temptation, for underneath the cabbages was a carpet of speedwell, and also a few rather weather-beaten dandelions. Further along Church Lane the ivy leaves on the old wooden fencing surrounding the churchyard were bright and shiny, with orange-red ladybirds out for a day in the sun.

The view is tremendous from the gate at the top of the hill leading down to the carrier. The tips of the twigs seemed to glow with new growth and new colour in the sunlight, the evergreen leaves and grasses shone. The colours, ranging from deep red to purple and orange, were muted as the ground steamed under the heat of the sun. With the smoke-like water vapour rising, it looked as though the roofs of the houses and the cut elms were on fire.

On reaching the bridge, we looked down into the river. The weed was being lashed from side to side in the fast-flowing current. The river was almost in flood, and the water quite brown with whirling silt depositing new banks, like underwater dunes, below the surface.

The reeds were completely white against the blue sky and the ancient water meadow drains were full. The ducks, mallards, flew to cover, while the moorhens scuttled away across the river, their feet barely touching the water, their wings flapping.

[38]

Dandelion.

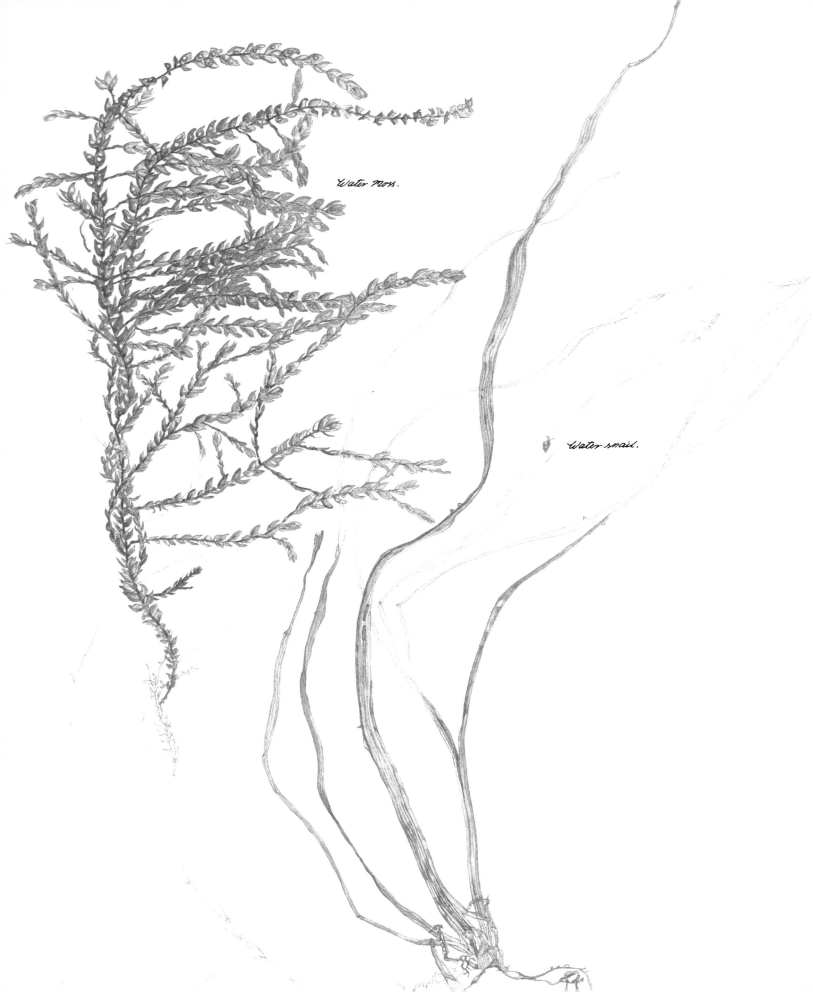

Water Moss.

Water snail.

The old farmyard-cum-Canada goose was
there, looking bored. He was inspecting his
domain with perhaps a tinge of despondency;
for he was no longer in the
field keeping watch for his
enormous gaggle of Canada geese, as all
of them have disappeared. He was now
back to his riverside haunt. Alerted to our
approach by the snapping dried reeds underfoot,
in a moment he was facing us, red beak slightly open,
safe in the knowledge that a wide river lay between us.
Suddenly we heard a swan, and saw him flying low towards us. Ten
yards in front of us he began his descent to the water's surface, wings
curved, the tips of the feathers pointing directly towards the river. The
sound of the rushing of air through his feathers was remarkably loud.
It was a very exciting and beautiful sight to watch and listen to a swan
touching down, webbed feet forward, just in front of us.
Whilst I was overawed, the goose was not; he was friendly with the swans
and their families, and lost no time in waddling in a somewhat ungainly
way into the water. He was giving a rather muted alarm call as he paddled
furiously to keep up with the swan. He perpetually grumbled away into
his ludicrous double chins when people were about.
The swan was unruffled by our footsteps on the bank and joined his family
further downstream, while the goose followed. There were four almost fully-
grown cygnets. I did hope that this was a different family from the one I had
seen last year, for then I watched *seven* young cygnets paddle down the river
in line, the cob in front, the pen bringing up the rear. Mr Fox often used to say
that a cygnet taken at the right time made a delicious meal with quince jelly,
and that all water-keepers tended to eat a few cygnets, as swans were a nuisance
and put down the fish. I was really appalled, but whether he was pulling my leg or
not, I'm not sure. We walked along to the old chestnut tree that grows beside the
bridge of old railway sleepers on the main river. The dry warm wood of the bridge is
covered with the most sumptuous mosses and lichens, contrasting with the torrent
of ice-cold, clear water that rushes and cascades beneath it. The water weeds
wiggle like snakes in the current; some water rushes along a deep man-made

[41]

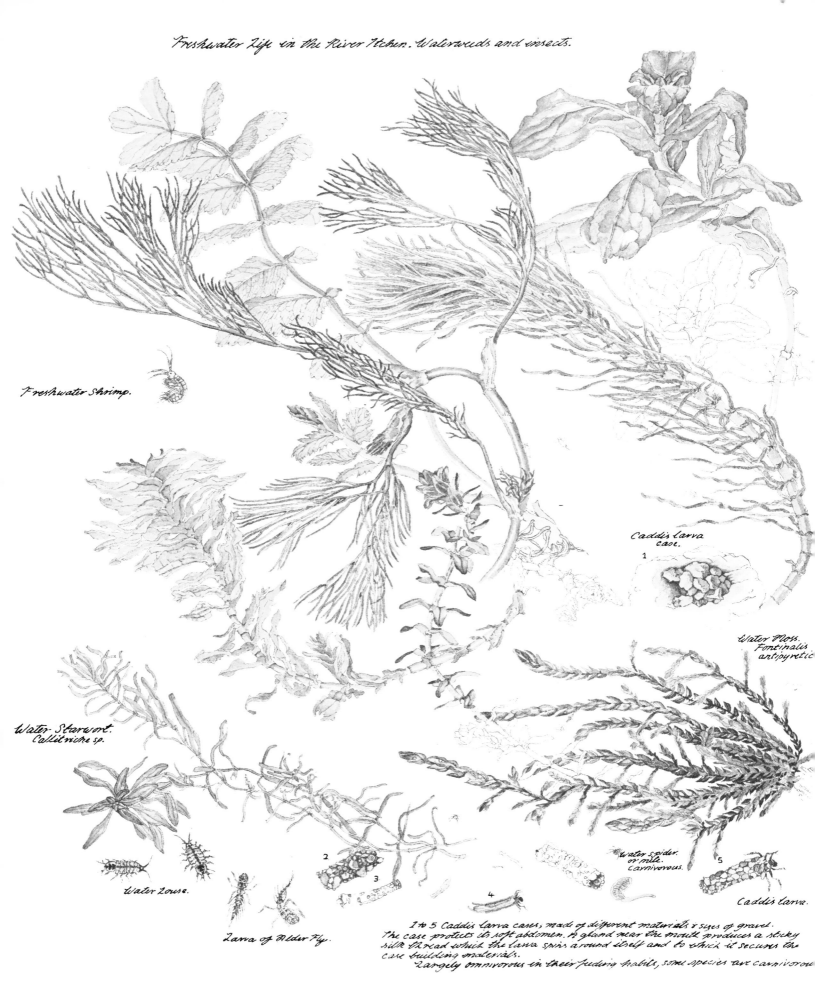

Freshwater Shrimp.

Caddis larva
case.

1

Water Moss.
Fontinalis
antipyretic

Water Starwort.
Callitriche sp.

Water louse.

Larva of Alder Fly.

2

3

water spider.
or mite.
carnivorous.

4

5

Caddis larva.

1 to 5 Caddis larva cases, made of different materials & sizes of gravel.
The case protects its soft abdomen. A gland near the mouth produces a sticky
silk thread which the larva spins around itself and to which it secures the
case building materials.
Largely omnivorous in their feeding habits, some species are carnivorous

trench on the right bank. The purpose of this is obvious, for an enormous rusting water-wheel stands in the centre of this stream. The wheel can now only be turned with effort and will-power; my husband gets the job while the world's laziest naturalist awaits the outcome, with a plastic bag. I have decided to collect as many species of water weed as possible and have learnt that this is by far the best and easiest way. Slowly the wheel is turned, and up come rich green clumps of intermingled emerald weeds. I pick my way amongst these eagerly; such designs and such clear bright colours! Some caddis larvae and their cases cling to the weeds and shrimps, a worm wriggles; I collect the best specimens and the wheel is turned again until the broken weeds and the creatures that live amongst them are again submerged.

March 12th
Although the weathermen predicted snow and sleet in March, I cannot remember one rainy day in the last two weeks. The sounds of lawn-mowers, tractors and birds herald the spring.

Last Tuesday I saw the most extraordinary thing. I was trying hard to talk to a very polite and kindly couple about a print that they wished to purchase, but my eyes were continually drawn to the window. In the end, ignoring the poor man's questions completely, I drew his attention to the extraordinary fierce battle taking place just beyond the window ledge. One large, glossy, female blackbird stood, head cocked to one side, watching two somewhat bedraggled female blackbirds fight until I was frightened that one of them might be seriously injured. The two birds went over and over, wings flapping on the grassy slope. Eventually one bird was actually standing on the breast of the other. The noise and wing flapping went on for a while, then stopped, Both birds faced one another, a distance of about four inches between them. Then they lowered themselves slowly on to their stomachs, opening their wings and flattening themselves against the ground in a menacing

[43]

fashion. One had a broken left wing, from a fight or an accident. Both birds kept their beaks open, and moved rhythmically, as if to start the battle again. But as suddenly as it had begun, the fight was over, and the two exhausted birds and the sleek spectator hopped away.

March 13th
Today I found a lichen, with the most wonderful bright red spores, on the railway sleeper bridge; I am almost positive that the spores were not there last week. I had spent a warm, sunny hour on Saturday inspecting the microcosm of life between the cracks and crannies of the bridge, each carpeted with velvety mosses, the spores and reindeer lichen reaching up to the sky. A tiny perfect world full of soft and vibrant colours, with some smooth glistening surfaces of 'cushion' mosses, some dry lichen, like antlers, dusty, pale and crinkled; and some yellow and orange lichen made of minute little cups. Tall, cool-green sphagnum moss grows in the deeper furrows, and I am tempted to use my father's microscope to make this dead wood and its inhabitants the sole object of my studies.

It may seem totally boring for most people to see paintings of tiny creatures and plants that they never have seen and never will see with the naked eye; for myself, however, the subject of life between the cracks and crannies of bridges appeals enormously.

March 16th
Started to paint the lichen with the red spores. I was quite fascinated by its form and colours. Today it is bright but bitterly cold, with the river blown into tiny white horses and driven against the bank. I saw a bird in the reeds with a tiny black head, but it flew away before I could identify it. A couple of partridges flew up in front of me, flying low across the field. Rooks seem to be everywhere at this time of year; there were as many as fifty in the nearby field. And there seems to be a vast population of moles this year, judging by recent activity.

The wind is fierce, and my ears are cold and sore, despite the woolly scarf tied firmly around my head. I turn for home and look nervously at donkey and horses. Horses do not come up to me when I have company, but when I am alone I seem doomed. I walked confidently, at least I tried to appear confident, up the winding cattle path, trying to make as little noise as possible. They all appeared to be engrossed in grass-munching, but that was as much a façade as my confident steps. Suddenly, one galloped towards me and the others followed suit – it was obviously some sort of game to them. I said 'Hello!' rather loudly, the blood rushing from my face into my wellington boots. Their eyes rolled; they snorted and I escaped, walking, then trotting, then breaking into a gallop. I cleared the stile with knees shaking, and a sense of profound relief.

March 18th
I went down to the river well wrapped up as it was a cold day. The willow twigs and young branches were more orange; the ash by the old brick bridge had swollen, dark purplish buds; the May bushes had tiny green closed buds and the pussy willows looked lovely with their pale yellow pollen.

   On one of the warmer mornings recently there was dew on the newly-cut grass of the children's playing field, and I saw a curious trail in the dew, fairly straight and a uniform ninety millimetres wide. I couldn't think what had made it. Then I saw a blackbird cock chasing another from his territory; his head was low, his body hunched and his tail feathers were spread out, rubbing the dew off the grass as he ran after the intruder.

APRIL

April 7th

My young brother-in-law, Johnny, arrived for a ten-day visit, meaning more washing up, more cooking, but a lot of shared interests. He came with newly-purchased bug-catching equipment, boxes, plastic bags and some superb camera equipment.

We set off for a walk in rather austere weather. Apart from Johnny, who happens to share my interest in natural history, I usually find myself on walks having to run to catch up with my friends, about every ten minutes. Now, I was able to spend two hours inspecting the ancient hedgerow at the top of the hill with a companion as interested as I.

He sucked up the few insects there were through a rubber tube into a large plastic tube. I made a mental note to obtain two bits of rubber tubing, a plastic tube and a filter, and to make this useful bit of equipment. We found one long black and orange insect, and one smaller creature with the same colouring, a pale duck-egg blue spider, a centipede and some rather hideous horse-fly-like insects.

We branched left into one of my favourite sheltered spots, where I hoped to find a flower or two and a few nests. This spot always excites me, surrounded by thirty-foot chalk cliffs that form a perfect semi-circle. Old man's beard cascades downwards and creeps along the ground. I remembered the mass of ancient wild roses in the summer, their stems as thick as my fist. Later had come the sloes with their beautiful purple bloom; and the rose hips, red and orange, large and brilliant.

I clambered up to look downwards into the old man's beard and, sure enough, there was a nest! It was last year's, very tatty, not unlike that of a wood pigeon, but it intrigued me to see that the ripe fruits of the clematis, with their silvery long awns, had been used to line it.

I also found an old thrush's nest and, was amazed to find four eggs. This still puzzles me; surely a squirrel, magpie, or even a rat would have eaten the abandoned eggs some time ago? Clearly a nest to watch.

Centipedes.

The deserted nest of a Song Thrush found in a holly hedge five foot from the ground. The nest is made from many different species of moss and some dried grass and sticks. It is lined with mud and fragments of rotten wood thus distinguishing it from the Blackbird's and Mistle Thrush's nest.

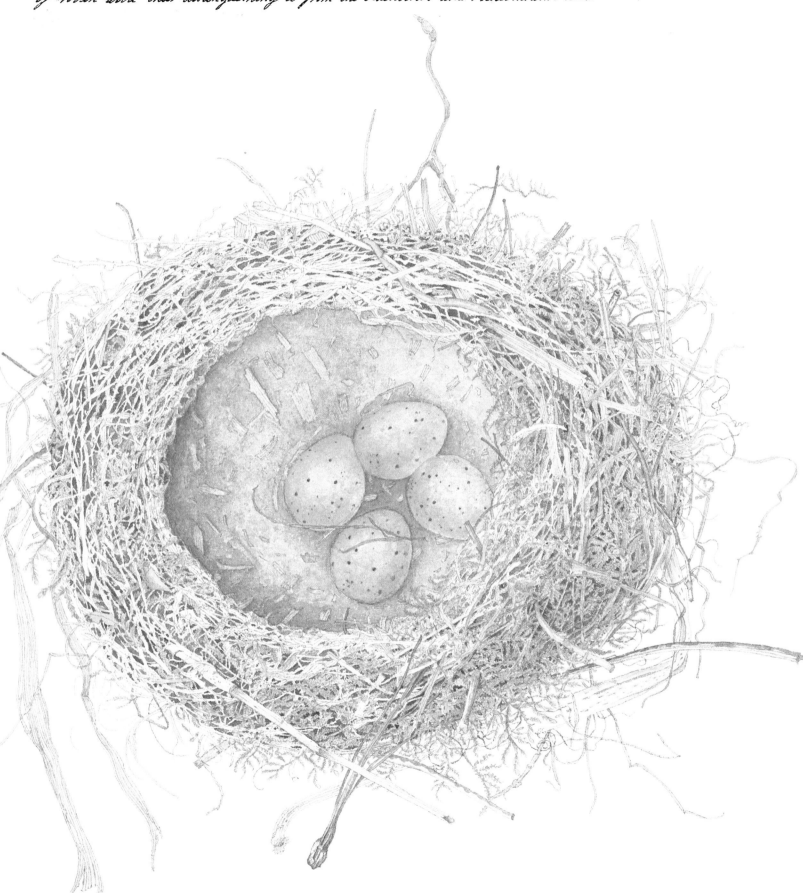

ladybird about to fly.

Only one flower was out, a sloe, everything being depressingly late on account of the weather. I clambered through the old man's beard and started looking for treasure in the shape of both china and glass. This hidden place had been the village dump in Victorian times, and was probably the dump as far back as the oldest houses in the village – ours being three hundred years old. With the aid of a stick, I laboriously dug down; everything seemed broken, but I eventually found one tiny horseshoe and one blue glass medicine-bottle stopper. Wonderful to indulge in a childish treasure hunt, I thought, and was determined not to be put off by a pair of teenage eyes looking at me.

"I'm not into that sort of thing," Johnny said, and I watched him flick away a mound of moss in a casual way. He bent down and to my amazement picked up the perfectly painted head of a china Victorian doll. From that moment he was hooked, and found wonderful glass phials and bottles, while I became steadily more disheartened.

It grew cold and we walked back, clanking with oddments, the wind stinging our ears.

April 9th

Cold, grey weekend; the weather throughout the end of last month and the beginning of this has been miserable; after the first hopeful signs of spring some weeks ago, the countryside has been spellbound, waiting for the warmth of the sun.

Found that the patch of butterbur was in flower near the Bush Inn, a nightmare to draw and paint. There are no leaves as yet, but they will follow the flowers and grow to a great size by the summer. Some say that it derives its name from the fact that the leaves were used to wrap up butter.

In the afternoon we visited Crab Wood again. It was cold and we were all wearing layers of jerseys, gloves, and woolly socks. Nothing much had changed. Dog's mercury still thick underfoot, intermingled with sweet violet, wood sorrel, wood anemone and masses of wood spurge. Unfortunately, none were in flower due to the cold weather; the flowers are pale green and they should have been out last month, but I think that

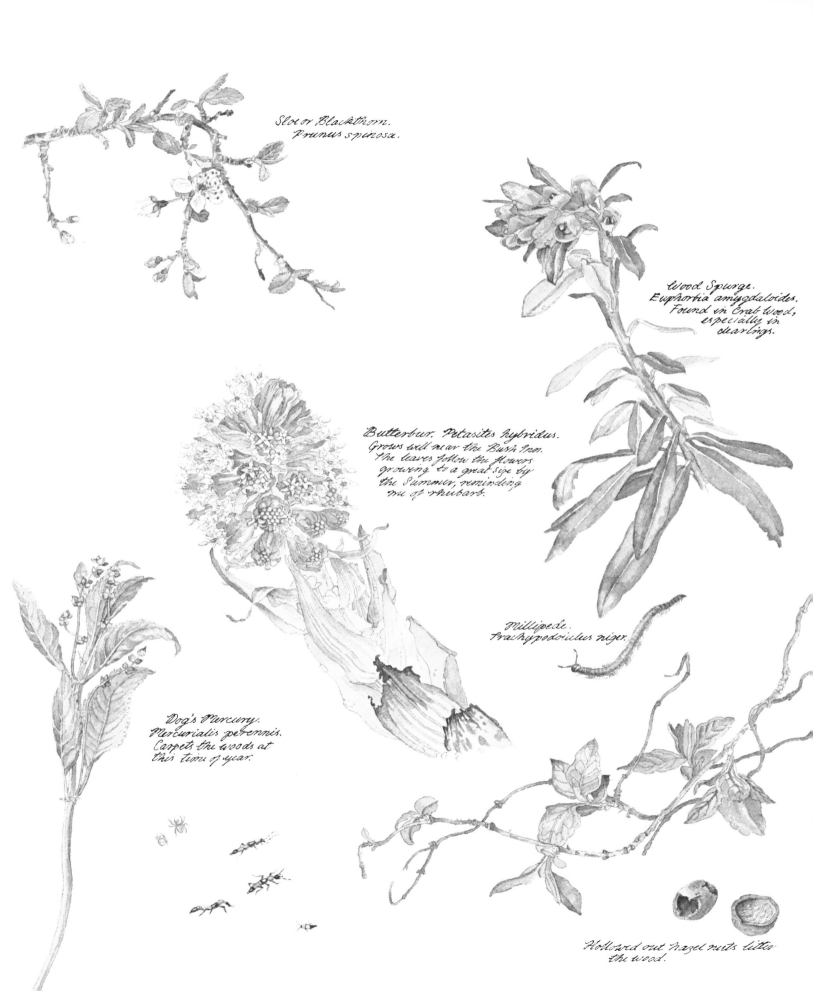

Sloe or Blackthorn.
Prunus spinosa.

Wood Spurge.
Euphorbia amygdaloides.
Found in Crab Wood,
especially in
clearings.

Butterbur. Petasites hybridus.
Grows well near the Bush Inn.
The leaves follow the flowers
growing to a great size by
the Summer, reminding
me of rhubarb.

Millipede.
Trachypodoiulus niger.

Dog's Mercury.
Mercurialis perennis.
Carpets the woods at
this time of year.

Hollowed out hazel nuts litter
the wood.

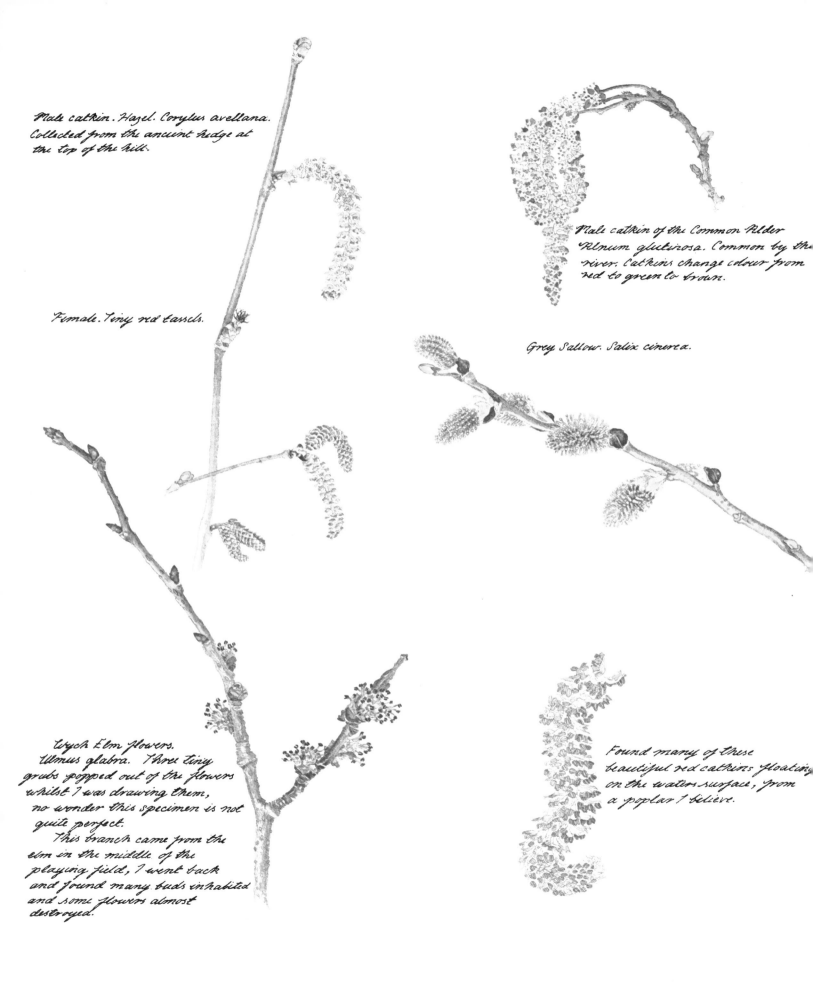

Male catkin. Hazel. Corylus avellana.
Collected from the ancient hedge at
the top of the hill.

Male catkin of the Common Alder
Alnum glutinosa. Common by the
river. Catkins change colour from
red to green to brown.

Female. Tiny red tassels.

Grey Sallow. Salix cinerea.

Wych Elm flowers.
Ulmus glabra. Three tiny
grubs popped out of the flowers
whilst I was drawing them,
no wonder this specimen is not
quite perfect.
    This branch came from the
elm in the middle of the
playing field, I went back
and found many buds inhabited
and some flowers almost
destroyed.

Found many of these
beautiful red catkins floating
on the waters surface, from
a poplar I believe.

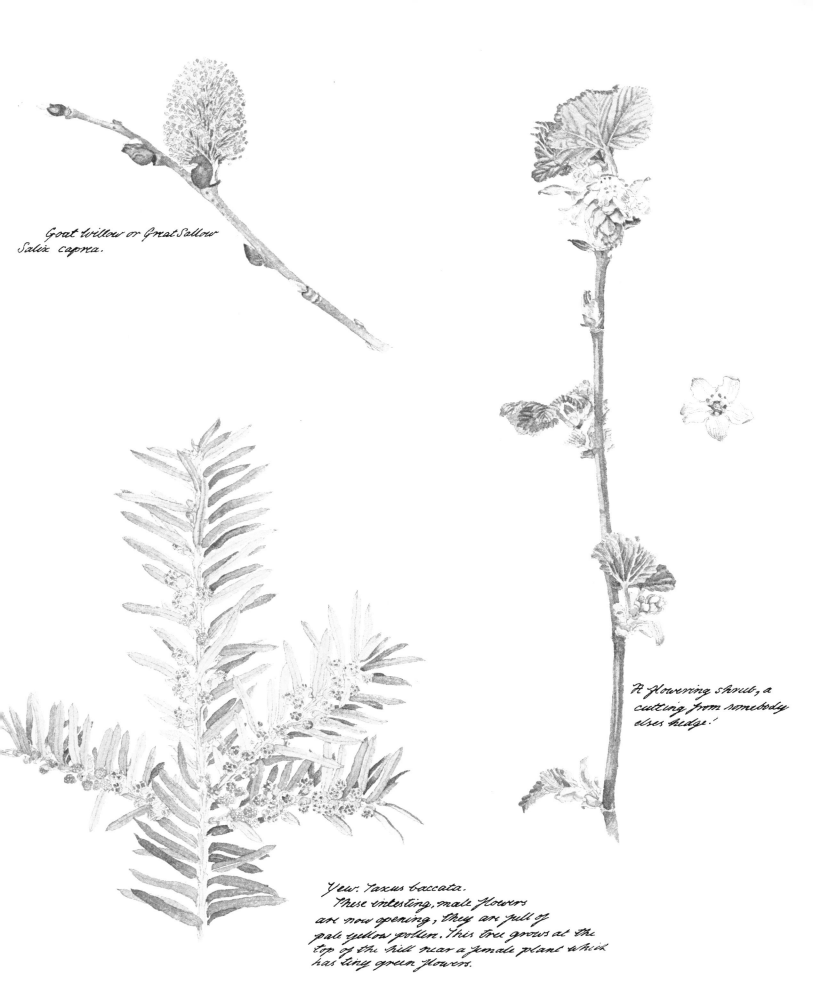

Goat Willow or Great Sallow
Salix caprea.

A flowering shrub, a
cutting from somebody
elses hedge!

Yew. Taxus baccata.
These interesting, male flowers
are now opening, they are full of
pale yellow pollen. This tree grows at the
top of the hill near a female plant which
has tiny green flowers.

it will be at least three weeks until they are in full bloom.

Dog's mercury is one of the most uninspiring plants I have ever seen, but I supposed it was important to record it visually. Pussy willows and catkins hang overhead, whilst primroses bespeckle the ground alongside the barren strawberry and dog violet; but still no real spring in the air, the hedgerows remain predominantly brown and bare.

April 10th
We all went to Crab Wood. Cold, wet day but still plenty of people wandering around this attractive nature reserve. The long, thin blue-red leaves of the wood spurge seemed to be everywhere; the pale green flowers were just beginning to show, but none were fully out. All in all, a wintry, wet, dull scene except for the vibrant green of the dog's mercury that carpeted the wood. A few violets showed their faces; and hazelnuts scattered the path, some cracked cleanly in two by squirrels, and others hollowed out and showing the tiny teeth-marks of mice. We soon lost heart in the heavy drizzle and walked rather briskly back to the car.

April 11th
We drove to the wood near Avington Park. Wet weather but an interesting wood. On the left of the road the wood consisted mainly of ancient yew and box trees which were both in flower; the box had tiny clusters of yellow flowers latticed against the dark green foliage. I found a marvellously-formed bracket fungus and on it were the most beautiful snails. They were dark brown, with shells that spiraled upwards to a pale brown point. When I first noticed one, I thought it was the chrysalis of a moth or a butterfly. Also on the same bracket fungus was a weird, pale-brown type of bug, with the most ungainly walk and a comical back view. Sharing this small world were a number of tiny black slugs with long horns, and some small black beetles. The moss and lichens in the wood were really exciting, the most fascinating being a pale, blue-grey-green lichen growing on a branch of horse chestnut tree. It was about the size of my fist and branched again and again from one stem into a woolly mass of what looked like soft hairs; in fact, it was surprisingly firm to the

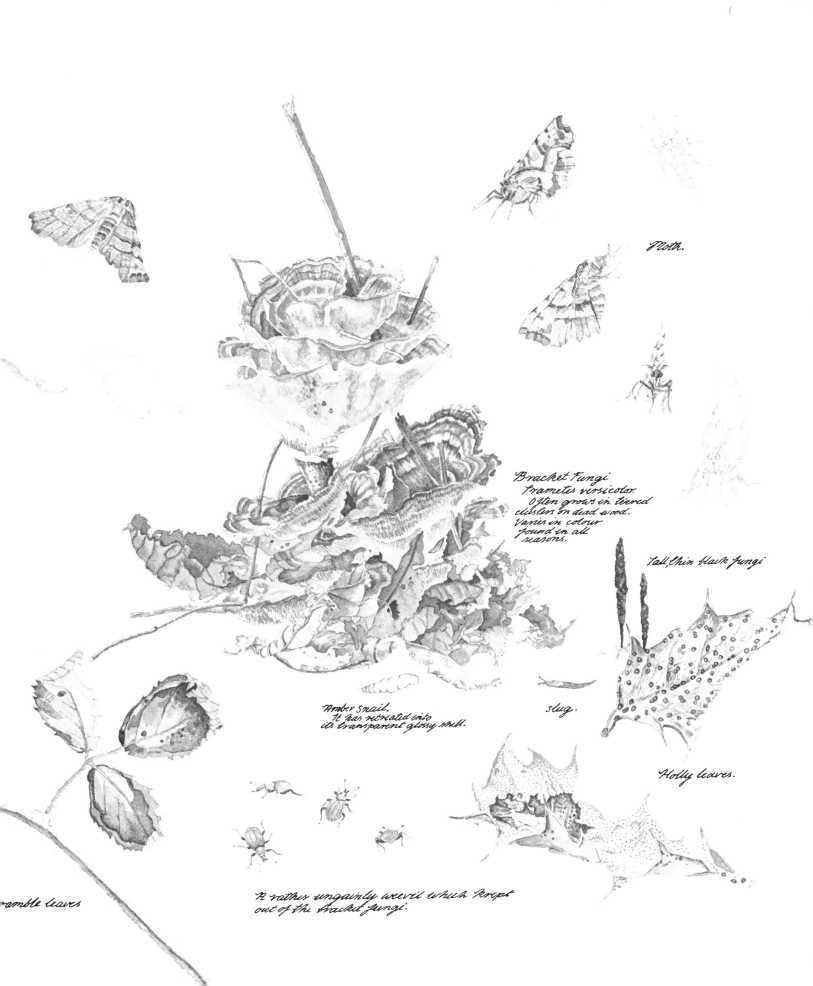

Moth.

Bracket Fungi
Prametus virsicolor.
Often grows in tiered
clusters on dead wood.
Varies in colour
found in all
seasons.

Tall, thin black fungi

Amber Snail.
It has retreated into
its transparent glossy shell.

slug.

Holly leaves.

ramble leaves

A rather ungainly weevil which kept
out of the bracket fungi.

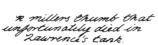

a millers thumb that unfortunately died in Lawrence's tank.

touch. Some fungi I had never seen before grew on a piece of moss-covered wood, they were about an inch high and looked like miniature, black poplar trees. Again, however, the weather broke and we were forced to retreat, thankful that rain was falling instead of the snow and hail of the last few days.

April 15th

Woke up to the first really sunny day in many weeks. Took my parents and the disobedient dog Fred with me to the river, but regretted it, as he upset both fish and wildlife. I had heard the cuckoo yesterday and today saw swallows whirling overhead. I was thrilled to see a beautiful male brimstone butterfly, and later in the day the pale female of the species. On the way down to the river I looked on the ivy-clad post near the churchyard for sunbathing ladybirds. They were out in force and accompanying them were two queen wasps, their black markings glistening in the sun. I took a photograph of the ivy's green sheen, covered with tiny red, and red-orange, bright ladybirds and yellow wasps. Again, I wished that I had had the correct lens.
Bright leaves clad the hedgerows and the dark bark of the hawthorn bush. Reeds and irises pushed upwards; some of the greens were emerald, others almost blue.
Squelching about in one of the many man-made waterways, I found a tiny island, an almost perfect square foot of texture, line and colour. Red shoots, little blue-green thistle plants and the beginnings of early marsh orchids encircled a tiny skeleton that had been left by some unknown predator. The skeleton was of a fish, easily recognisable as a miller's thumb. The whole of nature seemed to be summed up on that earth intricately threaded with both new life and death.
The kingcups, or marsh marigolds, are slowly coming into full bloom along the river bank, a few cuckoo flowers are in flower along the hedgerows; again, the old is intertwined with the new; the coarse, pale rushes thread their way under and over the big shiny green leaves of the plant growing up at their feet. Bees, hoverflies and many tiny black beetles interested themselves in the huge yellow flowers

[54]

eggs –

Lady's Smock or Cuckoo Flower.

and other early blossoms. One species of hoverfly had great smooth, orange sacks of pollen on his legs.

The snipe are still in evidence but no longer drumming in their display flight. The reason was soon apparent. A snipe got up at our feet and a search in a tuft of grass revealed a nest with four surprisingly large, dark-speckled eggs.

Earlier in the day we found a pheasant's nest with no fewer than eleven eggs of very varied colouration.

Spring was certainly advancing and the predators were already showing themselves. The kestrel was hovering over our heads and was later seen in laboured flight with a frog in his talons. Over the bridge spanning the main river, came the little brown form of the stoat. Bird life is now very active, with reed buntings sitting on the barbed wire, and both the pied and the grey wagtail darting over the water after flies.

A large number of black hawthorn flies are to be seen flying with trailing legs, just like miniature witches riding on broomsticks.

I discovered a trout, of about one and a half pounds, dead on the river-bank. The deep wounds on its back I thought at the time were almost certainly made by a heron. Why it left the fish after killing it and dragging it on to the bank, one can only conjecture. Perhaps the large trout was too big to swallow, or maybe the heron was disturbed.

On the way back I investigated an enormous clump of brambles, almost certain that there would be a nest and determined to see it before the green leaves made it impossible. The brambles decided to investigate me and I had great difficulty in extricating myself from the bush. However, I had been correct in my assumption; an old and a new thrush's nest existed between those enormous thorns.

The smell of newly-cut grass hit me as I neared the stile; I drank in that marvellous smell, and the sunshine and the sound of the birds. Nearing the gate, however, quite a different smell lingered and I looked for the plant responsible. In a triangle of waste land, between what was once the playing field and the road, grew a mass of wild garlic plants not yet in flower. Once in their midst, when the smell was overpowering, I found a

[59]

newly-shot wood pigeon, which I put in my carrier-bag to paint, perhaps also to eat. An aged willow grew in the corner of the plot, and tucked in a cleft in this enormous hollowed trunk was what looked like a new nest. I climbed up and then made the mistake of looking down before I had reached the nest. My head for heights used to be perfect as a child, but now I felt faint and timidly retreated.

April 23rd
I walked downstream towards the wooden bridge. It was about 12.30 pm and a fisherman was out for his first day of the fishing season. As I approached him, I could see by his bent rod that he had a trout on; the fish had gone into the weed and was gripping a frond with its teeth and was thus immovable. He tried pulling in both directions with the rod and line held straight out – to no avail. He then left the line slack and hoped the fish would let go. It did, but it managed to get the fly out of its mouth at the same time and he reeled in sadly.

Found a dead wood pigeon amongst the wild garlic

I continued towards the wooden bridge and saw a Canada goose sitting
on the bank across the river. The bird stretched its neck forward and kept
very still. I hoped that it was not a nesting bird, as its colouring, which is
ideal camouflage amongst rocks and melting snow, is not effective in
bright green grass. I crossed the bridge and walked along a sodden path
until I could look down the small waterway which runs left off the main
carrier, to see if the female Canada goose might be there on a small
island, nesting safely in the same place as she did last year. I could just
discern her. Her colouring hid her beautifully amongst the different
browns and fawns of the dead foliage; only the white patch under her
chin, which should be matching melting snow, sometimes gave her
away. The gander stays near his mate and keeps watch. The parents'
colouring is alike and they both look after the young.

I saw only one pair of mallard ducks fly up from the marshy land near
the goose's nest: one pair and five drakes. The drakes are very brightly
coloured while the ducks are dull browns. Apparently, when the male
and female differ so much in colouring, the male has little to do with the
bringing up of the young, the duck, only, being camouflaged. The
mallard drake after pairing and mating has no more to do with the
proceedings. He goes off with other drakes and leaves the duck to
incubate the eggs and bring up the chicks. This applies also to the pheasants
which breed in the reed beds between the Itchen and the carrier.

I returned to the fishing hut and heard the chiff-chaff, and then saw a
pair in the smaller ash tree. They were the first I have seen this year. A
pair of grey wagtails, looking lovely in their spring yellow, were flying
over the river and back catching insects, their long tails bobbing
violently on landing.

April 24th
For the first time this year, it is hot enough for shirt sleeves. I walked
down towards the old green caravan to observe the toads, which usually
mate in a small man-made, semi-circular inlet. Last year they had not
arrived but the year before there was a great number. The tiny male
externally fertilizes the long string of toad spawn by getting on to the

*Female pheasant
sitting quite still
on her nest.*

[61]

Cross-section of stem.

Sedge found near the river April 11.

large female's back. I used to get on the bank in the hot sun and watch them; often the female would have the burden of two males on her back. Whilst mating is going on, both male and female seem oblivious as to what is happening around them. I remember stroking the head of one toad, and it made no difference to his courtship. Perhaps that was the fatal mistake, for most mornings I would find a horrible sight awaiting me. The toads were being killed by an unknown predator; one by one bodies were strewn about, most of them only half eaten. The remaining toads were seemingly undeterred, but, when I swam near the bridge in late April, some toads floated by me, dead – I think it must have been exhaustion or lack of food, or both!

Today, I did find toads in this same spot but sadly every single one was a male. The first one I saw lay dead on the path. After a while, I decided to look for more toads in the carrier just outside their chosen mating area. I was both horrified and amazed on looking down to see a huge trout by my feet with its mouth wide open; it was shaking a large female toad slowly from side to side, and was holding her tightly with its needle-sharp teeth. The trout having gripped her belly, the toad was now quite dead, her long legs trailing in the water. The fish slowly moved away, swimming upstream with its prize to the opposite bank. The male toads just a few feet away were to be disappointed; but I had learned and seen something I would never forget.

April 25th

Another ornithological experience. I found the most perfect round lichen nest in the crook of a tree on the right of the little stone bridge. I watched it, and quite soon a female adult long-tailed tit hopped out of the hole which faced away from the path. The extraordinary thing is, I had never noticed it before; probably because it is at eye level. Somehow it is more difficult to see the obvious, and besides, I never look for nests of blue-grey lichen, for who would expect to find one?

I sat on the old wooden seat near the hut and watched from a respectful distance. The tits were still incubating the eggs and feeding of young had not yet started. Further down the river another excitement awaited me. I noticed a red-chested bird sitting on a post, and I sat down to watch it as it was obviously no robin. It was a male chaffinch which was behaving like a flycatcher. It rose in the air alongside two rather pale females of wishy-washy, yellow-breasted colouring, and then plummeted, as gracefully as a butterfly, turning its body from side to side to catch a fly. Very exciting, but, disappointingly, when I came to look for the toads, every single one had gone elsewhere to breed.

April 27th
As I walked along the carrier by the tall poplars I noticed that the buds were coming out on the lower branches, but the high branches still looked as though it was January. It was a lovely warm day, after a very cold winter and early spring. I heard and saw a chiff-chaff, and listened to a willow warbler; I think they only arrived a few days ago. I saw a house martin for the first time this year, catching flies high above the river. And I heard a redshank and saw him fly down the carrier and then round over the flighting ponds. One year I found a redshank's nest in the wet land and grazing ground between the two rivers, past the caravan and the fence.

The river looks as if it is still early in the year, for the water weed has only just started to grow. The reed beds are very wintry-looking too, pale straw-coloured. But the may trees are covered in tiny green leaves.

The swifts should be arriving around the first of May, and we have put three nest boxes for them on the east wall of the cottage. I have read that as they are communal roosters, there must be more than one box. The ruined thatched cottage, which many swifts nested in for years, was pulled down last year and we are worried that they will arrive and be desperate for somewhere to nest. Swifts do everything on the wing; one year I saw a pair mating high in the sky.

When the wind is in the south-east, as it is today, there is a very warm spot behind some brambles at the foot of the poplars where one can always find butterflies. Today there

[63]

Male toads awaiting females.

were a small tortoise-shell and a peacock there. It was curious because they chased one another about at great speed, going high up together and dashing down again, as generally only butterflies of the same species do.

April 29th
There was a terrible noise as I neared the field and passed the converted school house. Mr Tilney was at the bottom of his garden and I thought to myself, how odd to have such a decrepit lawn-mower. For about half an hour I watched and listened. There were three birds making a noise not unlike one of those wooden things you swing round and round at football matches. Leaving them rushing noisily from branch to branch, I went home to look them up. They were missel thrushes.

April 30th
Found the nest of a little grebe or dabchick on the riverside upstream from the brick bridge. They are very common little birds but shy and secretive. The female quietly slipped off the nest as I arrived, swimming underwater for some distance to avoid danger. I would have liked to have observed the building of this nest, for the upper half consisted entirely of water weed which both male and female (being diving water birds) had scooped from the bed of the river. Fresh weed almost covered the four eggs and would probably have done so entirely if she had not been taken by surprise. The eggs were very pale with a green tinge.

Under the chestnut tree, by the railway bridge, I must have surprised a predator – perhaps an otter, for on the bank lay a decapitated eel.

Further along the river I stood perfectly still to watch one of the most beautiful river creatures, the kingfisher. Within a few seconds it was gone again, the orange-red chest and bright blue-green feathers looked marvellous in the sun. It occurred to me that I had never heard it sing.

All along the river little bright blue shiny beetles sat on dried leaves, or mated. There must have been a hatch of them for they lined the river bank. There had also been a hatch of black spiders, which scurried everywhere between the mass of pale dried reeds.

[64]

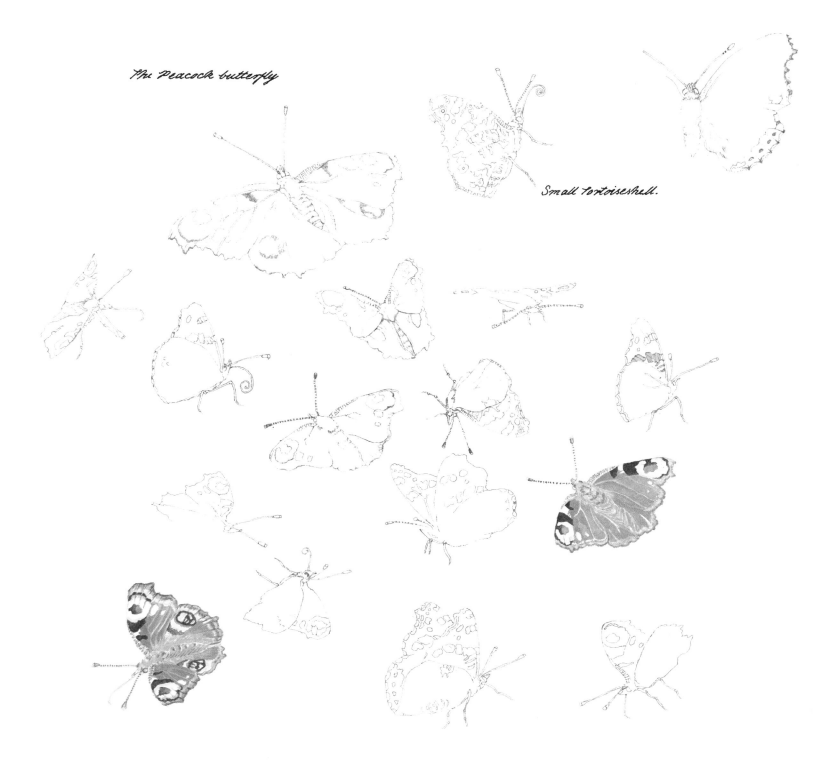

The Peacock butterfly

Small tortoiseshell.

Studies of butterflies feeding on the buddleja.

MAY

May 1st

It shouldn't rain on May Day, but of course it is pouring; and it was a wet and uneventful walk to the river.

It has been raining all night; the marsh marigolds, although in full bloom are, in the main, looking battered and unkempt, and the little man-made canals are filling up.

Three pairs of tufted duck were on the carrier, and two flew away, leaving one pair to guard their nest. I avoided that area and walked on; there in front of me, not twenty yards away, I saw a female mallard. She was obviously trying to lead me away from her nest. For about ten minutes we walked along at the same speed, while every now and then she would stop and turn her head to see if I was still following. Eventually, having achieved her object, she let out a cry and flew away.

I stopped on the bridge to see what was happening around me, what creatures were to be seen. Unfortunately, both animals and fish regard bridges as special places to watch out for and the observer is usually seen first unless he takes great care.

On this occasion, I was seen almost at once by a large bird, which flew swiftly down river. The conspicuous white wing, tail and rump suggested that it was probably a redshank, then his wild piping cry confirmed the identification. It was good to know that the redshanks were still nesting near the river. One year we found the nest, but have not recently come across one.

May 3rd

Walking quietly along the main river, I saw the first offspring of the year, a female mallard and her eight chicks. They looked like brown powder-puffs, their feet working away madly to keep up with the current.

The foliage of the yellow flag irises, which grow in such profusion in the ditches, crossed the meadow here in blue-green streaks. Water voles plopped into the water as I passed. In the evening, however, they appear not to notice me and sit on reed beds, their small, black close-set eyes watching fearlessly, as they pick up the odd lush green stems of grass and cut weed which have collected during the day. In the daylight hours, when undisturbed, they swim across the river with only half their bodies submerged, their fur glossy and red-brown. Even though I used a child's inflatable boat for many years to observe both birds and voles, I have never seen a vole and her young. I could watch them in their holes, chopping up grass into very small lengths (perhaps for flooring and bedding) quite easily with the aid of the boat, for the animals showed no fear of this floating object, merely a great deal of curiosity. At first the

bird life was fooled into thinking that I was a piece of driftwood. I would stop by stealthily, sinking my hand into the water and grasping as much weed as I could to hold me steady whilst watching the building of a nest in the weeds. A cold and tiring business for the arm, but fascinating even so.

But my boat, having been left in the hut for some time, had come to grief. One day I had decided to use it, but when I opened the door, there was an ominous smell of mice. Sure enough, when I moved the plastic boat two small heads popped up, their black eyes looked at me and in a second they were gone. Underneath the boat was an interesting nest made of grasses and leaves intertwined with pieces of orange plastic. I made a mental note to obtain another boat before this late spring is over.

Reed warbler.

May 5th
Spring is really gathering momentum. The horse chestnut leaves are a vivid green. May blossom covers the countryside here and there like a delicate cloak. Many trees and some hedgerows are still a little bare, as are the brambles; but I have seen my first buttercup in flower under the cabbages, and water avens, or billy's button, is in full flower by the river.

At least a couple of pairs of cuckoos call to each other in the valley every day. It must be extremely difficult for them in this late spring, firstly to find the woolly caterpillars on which to feed, and secondly to find a reed warbler's nest equipped with eggs in which to introduce their perfectly camouflaged, although larger, egg. The cuckoos we get in the valley are mainly reed warbler cuckoos; they have been born in tiny warblers' nests and their offspring and offspring's offspring will always remain reed warbler cuckoos.

Today I saw the first small white butterfly, having already seen the brimstone, peacock and small tortoise-shell. In this area, year after year, I have found that the beautiful brimstone is always the first to appear. Soon I hope to see the green-veined white and the orange-tip.

May 6th
Walking along the right of way between Chilland and Easton, where the

path crosses the valley, I saw a pen swan sitting on her eggs on a huge pile of twigs. The nest had been built up in a small backwater of the main river, well hidden by bushes and willows. She was asleep when I passed her, with her head tucked under her wing, while her mate was feeding nearby. When I returned, she was stretching her long neck down to the foot of her pile of twigs, straw and dried grasses, and pulling pieces up and placing them around her. I watched her do this for five minutes and she was still working hard rearranging things when I left.

On the bridge across the river on the same walk, I saw a chiff-chaff pulling hard at a cobweb which had been spun where the handrail met an upright. The web was strong, for the little bird had to pull very hard to tear some cobweb off; it then flew away with it triumphantly.

May 7th
Various flies were hatching on the water and were gratefully received by the fish. Their favourite fly today was the iron blue, a small fly which always hatches when the weather is blustery and cold.

Whilst I was watching along the bank I was confronted by the Canada geese; this time the pair were together, tending seven fine goslings. They had yellow heads and brownish bodies, giving an overall gingerish effect, quite unlike their elegant parents.

Returning to the fishing hut, I saw a pair of cuckoos, very hawk-like in flight, but the male giving his unmistakable call.

May 10th
Today I watched a pair of hawks wheeling higher and higher in the sky, sometimes skimming past each other. One stooped amongst a group of swallows and house-martins which were flying below them; but although it put its wings flat against its body and dropped like a stone, it did not attack them and immediately flew up again to circle with its mate. I think they were sparrow hawks, as they had broad wings and did not hover.

I have seen the swifts, who arrived on the 3rd of May, but I have seen no sign of them flying around the houses in the village looking for

[70]

nesting sites. As I was taking the dog for a walk along the lane, above the river that leads from Easton to Fulling Mill, I heard loud squeals coming from above me and saw the swifts swirling in the sky – it was about 3.30 pm on a sunny afternoon. Perhaps they do not nest as soon as they arrive, although they must do quite quickly for they are the first of the swallow family to leave again.

I saw the spotted flycatchers today; and they, the swifts and the fish were all very excited by a large hatch of medium olives. I got quite dizzy watching the swifts sweeping past the large may tree near the brick bridge, and down the river a short way before doing the circuit again. Now that the spotted flycatchers have arrived all the migrants are here.

May 13th
My grandmother died yesterday. It seems sad to die at this time of year when the countryside is so fresh and green. She loved the beauty of flowers and the countryside, and was an excellent water colourist.

Sunny day with a strong north-east wind. The wind was so strong that the only life I saw on the rough waters of the rivers was a pair of tufted duck near the lowest bridge of the carrier. As there was no sign of life, I went and sat with Fred in the reeds opposite the island where the goose had nested. The nest was finished with, as the young had hatched some while ago. It looked so untidy, wisps of down fluttering amongst a mass of droppings. Not far away was an old coot's nest which was tidy and clean by comparison. This nest was about eighteen inches above water – the water level having fallen after it had been built.

Swifts were chasing each other and squealing, disregarding the high wind. A pair of snipe flew overhead and landed in the water meadow between the main river and the carrier. A water vole was nibbling at pieces of weed, its beady eyes and whiskers glinting in the sun.

May 14th
Glad to see the pairs of partridges in the field on the way to Fulling Mill and by the river. But I remembered sadly that the nettles and so-called weeds had been twisted with paraquat along the hedgerows when I had

last walked that way. It would be even more difficult for the adult birds to feed their young on surrounding caterpillars this year. Their shape and their flight so near to the ground seem particularly ungainly; due to more and more intensive farming, they are decreasing in numbers alarmingly.

I noticed plenty of mallard and tufted duck in the flighting ponds but saw no nests. Blue shiny beetles again caught my eye along the bank, and spiders darted in and out of the reeds. There were water boatmen at the water's edge, something I had not noticed before, and many more young trout than ever before. The cattle-drink and newly-made 'island' were full of tiny silvery fish, swaying this way and that as if they were being pulled by the same invisible string. They leapt out of the water every so often; perhaps a predator was amongst them.

May 21st
7.30pm. The sun had been hot and blinding all day, but at this time of night the temperature is perfect, the countryside serene under the slight orange glow of the sun. The shadows from the white and green mushroom-like forms of may trees, are long, and the chalky path on which we walk has begun to crack like crazy paving, although the rest of the meadow and countryside in general are green and lush.

Each time that I go down to the river there is a different smell of summer; tonight, as the mist began to rise over the river, the rather oppressive smell of both may and cow-parsley flowers hung in the air. Nearing the river bank, however, there was a more refreshing smell – that of fresh water mint being trodden underfoot. The mint has grown very quickly in the last few days but is still nowhere near its flowering stage. On the left of the carrier is the flood plain, a most beautiful area, where an ancient man-made ditch, once part of the water-meadow flooding system, shows up against the yellow of the buttercups as a strip of blue-green. From early spring to early summer, this little bit of land has changed remarkably. At first, dandelions bespeckled the ground, then the beautiful orange-yellow of the marsh marigolds, then the daisies and now the buttercups. In

[72]

amongst the millions of bright yellow heads, there flowers one of my favourite plants – ragged robin – which is the second most common plant in flower in the meadow this week. By the river the bugle, dark blue in colour, flourishes alongside the water forget-me-not and water speedwell.

The weather has been very hot just lately, 80°F at midday. Plant life has therefore suddenly accelerated into growth and then flower, making life very difficult for the natural-history illustrator.

I watched Anthony fish from the little stone bridge; there were three large fish in the area, easily seen in the sunlight. We both concentrated our attention on one fish; from my position on the bridge I could see it clearly and study its movements, while giving instructions to the hopeful angler. To my surprise, the fish seemed to move around a great deal; I had always been led to believe that each fish had its own territory, that they faced upstream and ate any delectable fly that went past. My fish rose near the right bank, but very often it would move to the centre or the far left of the river, and feed.

As I walked away from the river, I heard shouts from the angler – the fish was on and was a big one. It was shaking its head from side to side and diving into the weed to get rid of this extra-tough fly. We let it go but, strangely enough, instead of retiring frightened and hurt it began to rise straight away in exactly the same position as before. I finally realised that fish were stupid after all, and went down river thinking of a delicious trout with hollandaise sauce and broccoli tips!

The coot was on her nest as I passed, the last of her eggs not yet hatched. The rest of her brood, completely bald, squeaked around the fallen branch, now and then clambering to her side. The male came to find them, but I did not see the regurgitating action, although I had seen

nymph.

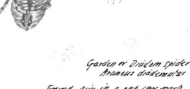

Garden or Diadem spider
Araneus diadematus

Found six in a pub car park,
one now this on my balcony.

him swallow, with a little difficulty, a miller's thumb.

I was surprised by the enormous amount of activity from the bumble bees at this time of night. It was 8pm and there seemed to be a great number of them taking nectar from the comfrey, for many other plants had already begun to fold their petals for the night. Diadem spiders sat minding their webs everywhere, but as yet there were few moths to be seen.

May 28th
The wild garlic is now in flower and seems to attract a lot of insects. Intermingled in this patch of strong-smelling white flowers are green alkanet, with their bright blue and mauve-pink flowers overshadowing the bluebells.

Lords and ladies, cuckoo pint or, as my grandmother called it, ladies' finger, is beginning to unfurl in the deep shade of the trees.

Daisies blossom on the right of the stile where the scullcap will eventually flower. And along the river bank, white and mauve-pink comfrey flowers droop their heads towards the water, which has become cloudy with silt due to the morning's heavy rain. Water avens are now in flower everywhere, the colour varying tremendously from deep strawberry-red to yellow to cream to white. The crimson-yellow rocket, or winter cress, has opened its yellow petals. The leaves, which had started growing in the autumn, taste bitter to me, but many people cut them up and eat them raw in salads; or they cook them. The caterpillars also find this plant a culinary delight, stripping the plant to the stem.

Some of the marvellously huge marsh marigold plants have now lost their heads. I noticed when drawing them that many of the flowers on various plants had six petals instead of the usual five.

The little grebe carefully pulled the fresh weed she had recently collected over her eggs and disappeared under the water as I neared the bend on the right of the carrier. The breeding or summer plumage of this little bird is very pretty, when she has chestnut cheeks and throat, and a white mark at the beginning of her bill. The rest of the plumage remains a brownish colour throughout the seasons.

[74]

A pair of tufted duck swam upstream from their nest, which is made of pale-yellow reeds resting on a piece of driftwood in the middle of the river. The eight eggs, white with speckles, blend well with the colour of last year's reeds. This duck has become more prevalent in the flighting ponds and along the carrier and main river. Pale-green and brown olive flies were abundant today, the fish again rising for them as I walked to the wooden bridge.

On the opposite bank I saw the eternal triangle, the white goose and two Canadian friends. Suddenly the male made a terrific noise and flew towards me, then landed in the water and feigned death. His neck stretched out on the water's surface, he drifted with the current. I had seen this last year, but then I had really thought that the bird was dead as it floated round the bend towards me and then out of sight. The bird feigns death to lead predators away from the nest – and a very good actor he is too. I walked away from the main river so as not to disturb him, but again he dive-bombed me and again somewhat noisily feigned death! In the end I headed away from the river towards the church, and a very cross goose actually got out of the water to see me off the premises! I got a good view of the

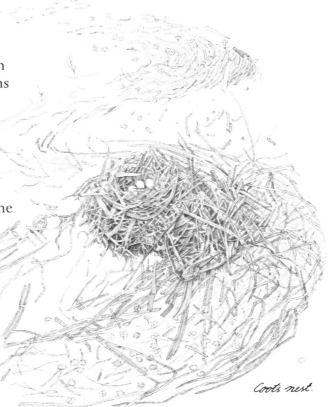

Coots nest.

[75]

goose's open beak and long rough tongue.

May 29th

Saw the Canada geese and their seven goslings. The goslings, now about a third of the size of their parents, have yellowish heads, and down of the same grey-brown colour as the adults. They all clambered up the river bank then stopped to graze. One parent, usually the gander, was on the watch all the time.

A mallard was coming downstream with her very young ducklings clustered round her, hugging the river bank. She was caught between me and the fisherman only a few yards upstream. She hid her young beneath an overhanging stumpy yew tree for a time; two young coot with red bills and white patches on their breasts were also there. The duck and her flotilla of dappled ducklings are very well camouflaged, as they carefully follow the contours of the river bank.

While walking from the Fulling Mill, along the very nettley right of way, I heard black caps and saw a female. I was also very glad to hear the cuckoo; once more he was in the clump of tall trees by the old brick bridge.

There are many pied wagtails feeding by the river; they effect amazing acrobatic movements to catch flies and are adept at catching more while they already have many in their beak. I watched one bird with a profusion of wings sticking out of its bill make off across the field to its nest. They do not seem to build near the river.

I saw a vivid yellow flash and watched a grey wagtail hen feeding a young one, who looked a pale but plumper edition of its mother.

One year the grey wagtails nested in the old water-wheel near the railway-sleeper bridge.

I heard and saw a snipe 'drumming'. I thought that this was only done early in the breeding season; but perhaps they are going to have a second brood. When walking back from the main river to the carrier, along the side of the reed bed, I heard an alarm call that sounded like a rusty wheel being turned rather quickly, and against the light I saw a brownish bird with a long slim bill sitting on a post. I think it was a

[76]

grey wagtail.

snipe, but I could not be sure, as the sun was setting in my eyes.

Two water voles swam by along the water's edge, one behind the other. It is the first time that I have seen two together; they generally swim about alone. They have several young a year, but those that are born in August do not survive the following winter.

Back view.

May 30th

The mustard fields look staggeringly beautiful, great strips of yellow on the hillsides. The chestnuts are in flower, the verges in a haze of white cow parsley, some six-foot high, the hedges a vivid green.

2.30pm. Walked down to the river. The alarm call of the pheasant came from every side, together with the constant call of the cuckoo. Cuckoo-spit brushes against my legs, the cause of it a tiny blue-green frog hopper nymph. The nymphal habit of living in a mass of white froth prevents the nymph from drying up and gives it a degree of protection against predators. When adult, this true bug has a frog-like appearance and tremendous leaping ability.

The white carpet of daisies and the wonderful array of different grasses particularly struck me. I gathered a bunch with great care to study and draw. Sat down and watched the trout rise in the clear sunlit river and suck in olive flies from the surface of the water. The colour variations between the fishes struck me. There must have been a recent hatch of male and female orange-tips, for they were everywhere, whereas peacocks and admirals were a less common sight today. The sun is hot, insects droned, the little dull-brown beetles were mating. Certain species of spiders have made little pockets of web in last year's dried vegetation, and sometimes the spiders can be found inside these pockets. The garden, or diadem spider lies in wait on his web for the tiny sound and movement indicating the ensnaring of a small insect. Why spiders, or indeed fish, bother with nymphs I do not know – one would doubt there was enough 'meat' on them. Delicate orange, yellow and black hoverflies move from flower to flower. A predominantly orange bumble bee making more noise about his travel, almost disappears up the

yellow.

Sketching antennae upwards.

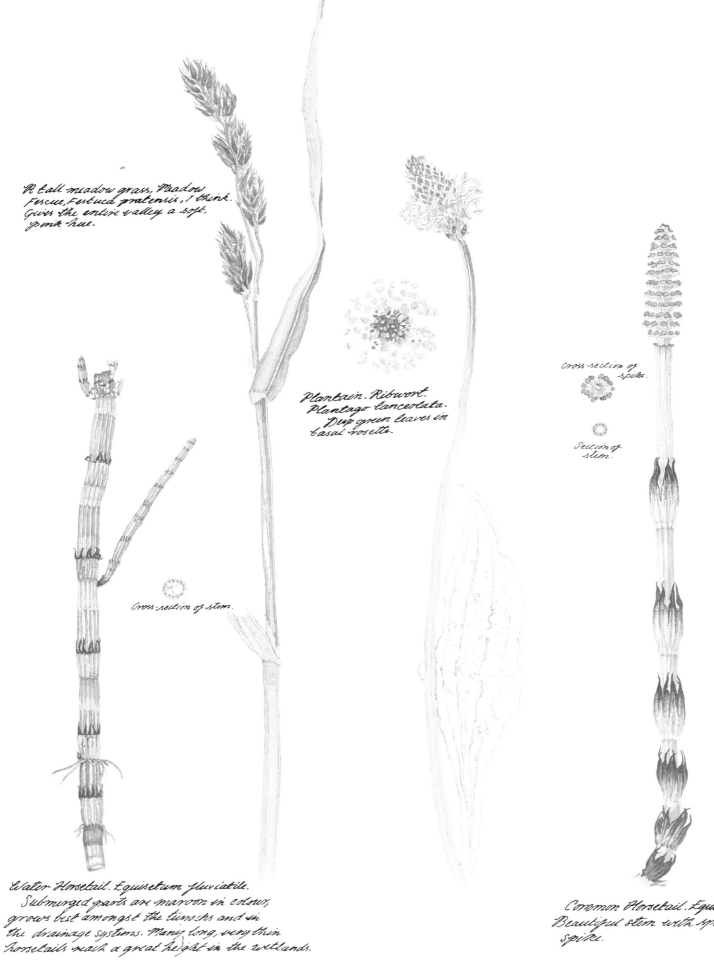

A tall meadow grass, Meadow
Fescue, Festuca pratensis, I think.
Gives the entire valley a soft,
pink hue.

Plantain. Ribwort.
Plantago lanceolata.
Deep green leaves in
basal rosette.

Cross-section of
spike.

Section of
stem.

Cross-section of stem.

Water Horsetail. Equisetum fluviatile.
 Submerged parts are maroon in colour,
grows best amongst the tussocks and in
the drainage systems. Many long, very thin
horsetails reach a great height in the wetlands.

Common Horsetail. Equisetum arvense.
Beautiful stem with spore bearing
spike.

Cowslip
Rare due to over picking

Common sedge

Hedge Bindweed or Bellbine
Calystegia sepium.

Currant or Magpie Moth.
Abraxas grossulariata.

Spear Thistle
Cirsium vulgare.

Scarlet Pimpernel or
Shepherd's Weatherglass.

comfrey flowers, with their blue, mauve and white bells.

The many different species of thistle are now no longer like beautiful mauve star patterns, flat against the ground, but are rising up towards the sky. The dandelions have reached the stage when they become delicate clocks; I plucked one and blew it in order to tell the time.

The clover flower is not yet out but in two or three days time it will burst into blossom, to the delight of those red-tailed bumble bees predominant in the area, and all the many different flies. No other new plant has opened its petals since I left two weeks ago, but the flower of the buttercup is now abundant.

8.30pm. Went with Anthony to watch him fish. The light was just beginning to fail, the cold night air sweeping across the valley in place of the dusty heat of the day. I inspected the ground at my feet and saw that almost every bluish blade of the yellow flag iris was host to a slug. Walking slowly, I saw slugs of every description, from tiny pale-brown creatures to the large black slugs with wonderful 'horns'. Tiny black moth-like insects with brown heads clung to overhanging grasses, and somewhere in the distance a very loud cricket-like noise pervaded the atmosphere. It was an incredibly peaceful evening; and I was able to watch the water vole, on a nearby water crowfoot and weed pad, chewing up lengths of stalk. The swans were dipping their long necks into the water, quite unconcerned at my presence; they showed up well in the fading light. I was hoping to see the ghostly sight of the barn owl, as it glides noiselessly downstream looking at the banks for voles and mice. I did not see the owl but I was able to watch the bats as they darted to and fro across the river. As we left, the mist began to rise, enveloping the swans and reeds.

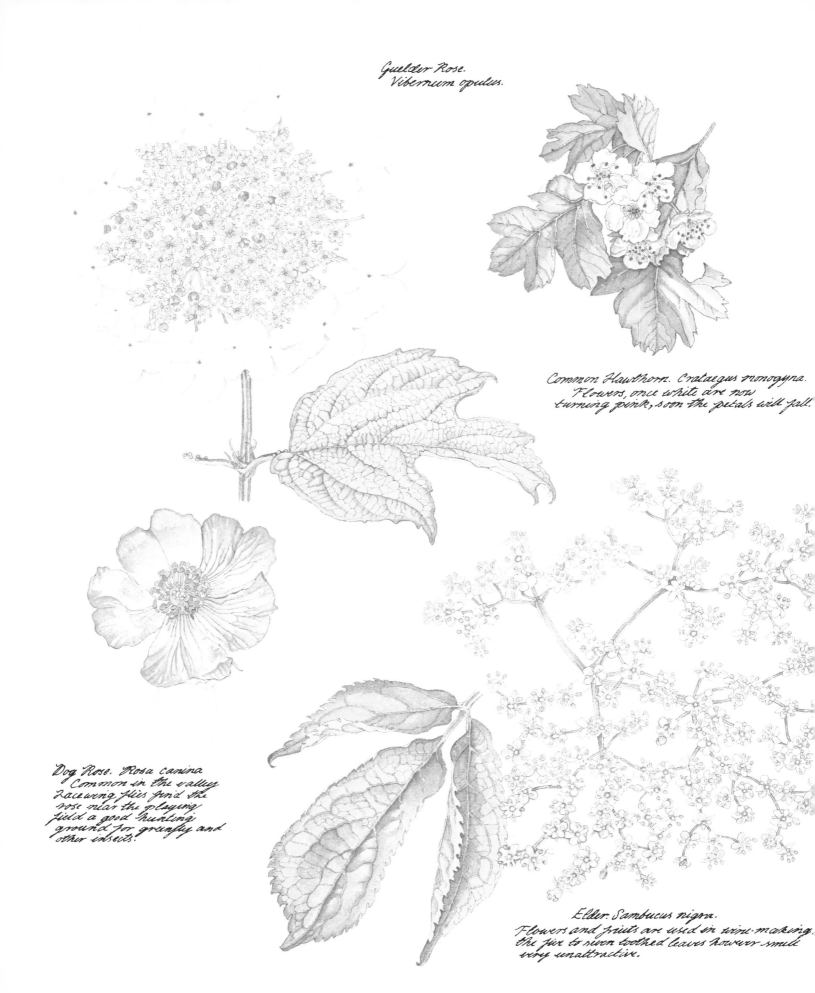

Guelder Rose.
Viburnum opulus.

Common Hawthorn. Crataegus monogyna.
Flowers, once white are now
turning pink, soon the petals will fall.

Dog Rose. Rosa canina
Common in the valley
Lacewing flies find the
rose near the playing
field a good hunting
ground for greenfly and
other insects.

Elder. Sambucus nigra.
Flowers and fruits are used in wine-making.
the five to seven toothed leaves however smell
very unattractive.

JUNE

June 2nd

8.00 pm. Watched Anthony catch a small fish, which we intended to put back immediately. On closer inspection, we saw that the fish had a great jaw-mark across its side, almost certainly inflicted by a pike. The wound was fairly fresh and we were surprised that it had lived at all, let alone be rising still for flies, for it could not have had long to live. In fact, owing to its wounds, it had about two seconds to live and we ate it for supper!

I went for a quick walk along the main river and saw the rather unusual sight of small fry jumping out of the water. They looked like little silver bars of light about an inch long, all jumping in quick succession to catch tiny midges on or just above the water's surface.

June 4th

2.00pm. Walked down the main road on my way to the large stone bridge. Picked some guelder rose to draw and some elderberry flowers. It gave me a headache to think of all the drawing that would be involved, hundreds and hundreds of tiny white petals and stamens. I looked at the elderberry flowers and was surprised to find that some of the flowers had four stamens whereas others had five.

Watched the river rushing through the arches of the bridge, the water crowfoot bobbing with the current. When I got over the stile into the field on my way to the river bank, I heard angry cries from the lapwings, or peewits, about a hundred yards from me. They reminded me of the two cockatiels we once bought to accompany William, our free-range, blue-fronted Amazon parrot. He used to wander up to them and throw them off balance by lifting up their tails. Eventually, he pulled out some tail feathers and we had no alternative but to move them to Dulwich Aviary.

I assumed that the peewits had nested near the man-made waterways

[83]

running across the field, so I got under the barbed wire to walk along the river bank. Immediately, the birds flew up into the air and, making an enormous amount of noise, mobbed me. I stopped, and there at my feet, making tiny cheeping sounds, was an enchanting peewit chick. On looking around me I saw six or seven wandering unsteadily about in different parts of the field, obviously without parental control. The small chick had large black eyes, long black beak, and long legs with large feet. Its little body was downy, and mottled with pale and dark brown markings. I moved along the bank quickly, to avoid disturbing the birds further, and saw a more sensible chick which had flattened itself on the grass and made no sound.

Peewit.

Thirteen Canada geese, plus six young born to the pair that stayed behind with the old white goose, cropped the next field.

The plant life along the main river is a little different from life in the carrier's meadow. Buttercups and ragged robin are less common and there are no bugles in the upper stretches. There is, however, a profusion of silverweed with its long runners rooting at leaf junctions. Some of these beautiful silver, toothed leaves can grow to about twelve inches in height near the water's edge, whereas others are the size of my little finger. The solitary flowers are a bright yellow, contrasting with the remarkable silver leaves. About one quarter of this field seems to be devoted to marsh horsetail.

Suddenly a peewit landed a few feet from me and commenced his big act, dragging one wing across the grass and then both, limping and staggering desperately as it tried to lead me away. I succumbed and followed it, past the now pink and ageing may flowers to the gate.

June 11th

Two female mallards and their young swam away from me to the other bank; they still have five chicks each, but the mortality rate of these tiny birds is very high. I can still hear the peewits in the distance as the swans feed quietly with their one cygnet on the carrier. Unfortunately, the water-keepers take many of the eggs as the swan is meant to be a nuisance to the fisherman.

I sat down in the meadow with paper, paint and brushes. I wanted to capture the strange green of the yellow flag irises, which are just showing their yellow buds. It was also the buttercups that attracted me to this spot – once a man-made waterway, and now a river of yellow flags stretching across the meadow, surrounded by golden heads of buttercups.

Life seemed to be particularly busy on the main river today. I went down in the afternoon after the morning's heavy rain. The swifts, with their strong curved wings, were speeding low – up, down and around the water, taking flies as they hatched; swallows and house martins, with their white rumps and white under-parts, were flashing to and fro amongst them. I tried to see the birds actually catching the flies, but it all happened far too quickly. I then saw a bird moving slowly up the river bank, hopping like a sparrow. It was a cock reed bunting. Its beak was already full of flies and every now and then it flew a yard or so over the river to take a fly actually off the surface film.

I saw a little grebe or dabchick being swept down by the current, with a large piece of weed in its beak. It dived on seeing me, and appeared yards down the river still with the weed in its beak. The bird did this several times and, when it had gone about a hundred yards from where I first saw it, I began to worry in case something was stuck in its throat.

Silverweed

[85]

Then I saw it approach three slightly smaller birds and hand the weed over to them; they fell on it greedily while the parent bird swam across the river towards a fourth young one, who came up to investigate but found the beak empty. It must have been a very special piece of food to have been carried so far with such care.

As I approached two fishermen near the chestnut-tree bridge, there was the noise of alarmed young birds, and a fledgling wren shot out of a bramble bush on to the shoulder of one of the fishermen, and remained there for some time. The fisherman was all in green and did not even notice as the bird was so light. The wren flew into a real tree later.

I saw the seven Canada goslings and hardly recognised them, as they now look like slightly smaller editions of their parents. They were all grazing, with one parent still constantly on watch.

June 13th
Yesterday, just as I was starting out along the lane to the church, I saw a hedgehog in the grass verge, curled up and breathing very slowly. At first I thought it was dead, and supposed it had been run over and had just managed to crawl to the roadside. I covered it with wet grasses – there was no dry herbage anywhere because of the rain. I looked for it again this morning, and found it had moved a short distance. It was still curled, though I could see its face and nose, and it was still breathing slowly. Perhaps it is hibernating again because of the cold wet weather.

June 14th
A really warm day; the sun is shining at last. At about 3.30pm I watched birds sunbathing. First a hedge sparrow settled on a dry sandy place where the ground was sun-scorched; it preened for a short time, fluffed its feathers and then lifted its wing so that the sun's rays could reach the maximum body surface. Then a cock blackbird went through the same procedure, but on finally settling down it opened its beak as well. It was not because the bird was panting, for it had not done this before settling down to bask; it immediately shut it again on being

Hedgehog

[86]

disturbed. Later I saw two other birds sunbathing on the branch of a tree in an otherwise shady spot. They were a cock chaffinch and another cock blackbird; this blackbird had also got his beak open, but like the other he closed it at once on being disturbed.

June 17th

Worked on my exhibition in Easton, which is to be part of the village flower festival, the money going towards the new church organ. Spent today painting the screens on which I am to clip my illustrations.

5.00pm. Walked along the carrier. The may flower is now over and the buttercups have almost disappeared. The yellow flag was, however, in full bloom; the line of both stem and leaf is beautiful. Along the riverside, the bittersweet is now growing in profusion, the first purple and yellow flowers beginning to open. The water forget-me-not is now in full bloom; very few of the pink buds remain. The marsh orchids, both large and small, are an inspiring sight; before the flowers are fully open at the tip, the look of the plant reminds me of asparagus.

Found yet another eel on the bank, again decapitated; the otter is responsible and has been seen further downstream.

The cow parsley has now finished flowering and the hogweed is about to take over. The hedgerows are intertwined with wild roses, and on closer inspection I saw seven or eight lacewings with shiny blue wings and green bodies flutter from one leaf to another. Their flight seems rather slow and weaving, and it is easy to see all four wings beating. Some actually stand on a petal but quickly move behind the flower, looking for aphids to eat. This little creature with its large red-brown eyes is my favourite insect.

June 18th

The hedgehog has gone. As I came into the children's field this afternoon I saw a green woodpecker fly down and start feeding near a newly-planted sweet chestnut tree. A second or two later a spotted woodpecker landed on the tree trunk and looked at the other bird to see what he had found. Having seen nothing of interest he flew off, followed

[87]

Stag Beetle.
Lucanus cervus. Male.

Found by Mrs Farley's sister in law on a pavement in town. She bought something at Woolworths, thus gaining a paper bag in which the beetle rustled until it got to my door. A very kind act for it's a beautiful beetle to draw and paint.

It escaped under the sofa and was only found by following the parrots horrified gaze as it came out and wandered across the carpet.

The jaws of the male are so large that they cannot be moved with any power, the females can give a stronger bite. They breed in rotting wood and sadly are getting rather rare.

Monkey-Flower. Mimulus guttatus.
An introduced perennial, naturalised and growing in profusion along
the river banks. Caterpillars seem to adore it, the leaves are said to be good
to eat, I find them rather tough and bitter.

Southern Marsh Orchid.
Dactylorhiza praetermissa.
Colour varies from cream to purple,
The valley is carpeted with
orchids this year.

Scarlet Tiger Moth.
Callimorpha dominula.

Creeping Cinquefoil.
Potentilla reptans.
Common amongst riverside vegetation,
cascading to the waters edge
near the wooden bridge.

Self-Heal
Prunella vulg

Forget me not
Myosotis arvensis.
Large forgetmenots
bespeckle the river bank.

Common Sorrel. Rumex acetosa
Found in abundance in the water meadows.
Can be used in a sauce instead of lemon, delicious
in sandwiches.

Common Quaking Grass.
Briza Media.
Giving a delicate mauve hue
to the valley.

Hover-Fly.
Syrphus ribesii.

Broad-leaved
Marsh Orchid
Dactylorhiza
majalis.
I think!

Red Clover.
Trifolium pratense.

The Spinach Moth.
gris mellinata.

by the green woodpecker.

I have often noticed that birds of a different species will come down to see what others have found to eat. I saw two starlings sorting out sticks with a view to nest-building, and a pair of pigeons arrived beside them to investigate before flying off again.

Weed-cutting is in progress and the river is strewn with rafts of ensnared weed, giving it a most untidy appearance. The water voles, however, exploit the situation and can often be seen sitting on a weed raft, busily engaged in munching the cut stems.

Low over the river fly the swifts, house martins and swallows, feeding mainly on a large yellow fly, which fishermen call yellow sally. And round the bend of the main river came a family of coots, the adult birds giving their shrill alarm call like the grating of a slate pencil. The harsh, though varied song of the reed and sedge warblers contrasts with the sweeter strains of the chiff-chaff.

Whilst watching the bridge over the main river, I saw a family of stoats cross rapidly. It is often rewarding to watch bridges over a river, as a variety of creatures make use of them. The hare also frequently uses the bridge by the caravan. On one occasion I noticed the hare making for the bridge and wondered what he would do, as the water-keeper was standing on it talking to a friend. Some five minutes later I heard splashing and saw a largish animal trying to emerge from the river, but having difficulty owing to the wooden wharfing. At first I thought it was an otter. When the animal finally landed further downstream, he shook himself, pricked up his ears and there was the hare.

The recent rains have encouraged a most luxuriant growth of vegetation. The marsh orchids are out, and many of the plants in the reed beds are shoulder high.

The yellow flag irises are still in flower but they are now joined by yellow rattle.

June 19th
The weather was strange today, for although there was a very strong north-east wind, it was much warmer than it's been in the last few days.

[90]

Drawings of mute swans and cygnets.

A. Water Forget-me-not. Myosotis
scorpioides. A beautiful design; I am
unable to capture the brilliance of
colour.

B. Water Avens or Billy's Button.
Geum rivale.
   Flowers usually pale pink,
however I have found both
strawberry red and white flowers.

C. Bugle. Ajuga repans.
   Grows especially well in the
cabbage field, also along
hedgerows and along the river
bank.

D. Cinnabar Moth. Tyria jacobaeae.
   I have also painted the black
and orange caterpillar.

E. Silverweed. Potentilla anserina.
Has beautiful silver leaves, on
rare occasions I have seen the
leaves amongst tussock 1ft. high,
normal height 15. cm.

G. Ragged Robin. Lychnis-flos-cuculi

F. Chalk-Stream Water Crowfoot.
   Ranunculus penicillatus.
      The river was literally carpeted with
these delicate white flowers this year.

Fred and I walked past the fishing hut to the main river and I was amazed to see how rough it was, impossible for fishing. The swans swam by with one little grey-brown form tucked in beside its mother. The two parents were close together and their necks and heads formed a perfect arch.

I climbed over the fence and walked through the water meadow. I put Fred on a lead, for there are young pheasants about and he is very good at finding them. As I walked through the gate towards the caravan, the sun came out and that piece of grassland looked beautiful, the mauve-pink grass heads blending with the brick-red of the sorrel and the occasional dark purple of newly-blossoming thistles.

I sat for a while with the fishermen on the seat by the tin tool-shed, opposite a big clump of water forget-me-not. We saw a pair of reed buntings; there seem to be many more of them this year. The fisherman then wandered off and Fred and I went into the flighting area behind the carrier. After about a quarter of an hour, the creatures came out of the reeds; a coot, a moorhen feeding daintily as it walked on the flowering water crowfoot, and two water voles. One of the voles cut off a piece of the riverside herbage and carried it triumphantly to the island, which was riddled with vole-holes. The swifts were hunting all around me, the high wind seemed to make little difference to their glorious flight; sometimes they came so close that I heard the wind through their wings. A snipe did not have nearly so easy a time against the wind; several times he rose up, and his quick wing beats were faster than ever, but he then went back to the water meadow.

I went to the fishing hut and heard the twittering of the family of long-tailed tits all around me. I watched wrens going busily to and fro into the hedge across the river; they must have a nest there. Then suddenly I saw a hawk fly into one of the larger may trees in the field. The hawk seemed paler than a kestrel, with a long tail but not very rounded wings.

June 25th
In Church Lane I saw a hen blackbird pulling hard at a large clump of seeding common chickweed. I thought she was getting material for her

nest but, having given the tangled mass a good pull, she then ate the seeds that had fallen off before giving the plant another good shaking.

I was astonished to see a mole crossing the road, a vulnerable, rather ungainly creature on the tarmac.

Walked from the road to the main river and heard a small noise which appeared to come from a tussock at the water's edge. Sure enough, I found a well-camouflaged and beautifully-woven nest. Inside the shallow nest was the last of the young with its tiny red bald head and orange neck feathers. I looked down at the little creature, wondering how this family had ever been raised on the river bank with so many predators to hand.

The male coot paddled closer to the nest and gave some rather startling calls to persuade the tiny coot to negotiate the big drop to the water.

Found the most beautiful marsh orchid by the telegraph post and determined to draw it.

June 26th
Went to put up the small exhibition of my illustrations; the flower festival begins on Friday. I hung pictures with difficulty.

June 27th
Today, however, was *the* day. Hair had to be washed, face made to look better, clothes, paint brushes, paper with drawings, hat, had all to be sorted out. This was followed by a large gin and tonic.

June 28th
This is the last day of weed cutting, and water-keepers are now busily trimming the banks and helping to move the accumulated rafts of weed downstream. This particular weed-cut must have been quite severe because the water level has dropped at least four inches, which is a lot for a chalk stream.

June 30th
The flower festival opened and looked quite promising; alas no cake stall!

[94]

1. *Green-veined White. Pieris napi.*

2. *Brimstone. Gonepteryx rhamni.* This is a male, the female is surprisingly pale, often mistaken for the Cabbage White although the Brimstone has a stronger and more direct flight pattern.

3. *Small Magpie. Eurrhypara hortulata.* 4. *Hedge Brown. Maniola tithonus.*

5. *Six-spot Burnet. Zygaena filipendulae.*

6. *Grasshoppers. Acrididae.* Top left, female grasshopper, I was lucky enough to watch her deposit an egg-pod which will protect the batch of eggs enclosed throughout the winter. 7. *Mole. Talpa europaea.*

JULY

July 1st

Walked down to the river in weak sunshine. The thistles are tall in the meadow, the pretty flower of the yellow flag iris is almost over, and the marsh orchids which grew across the meadows like a blanket looked ragged and faded.

The yellow and purple loosestrife are in bud by the river. Meadowsweet, with its feathery white flowers and pungent scent, was everywhere; the bright red buds and yellow flowers of the 'eggs and bacon' plant and creeping jenny were underfoot, the pink and white flowers of the bramble bespeckled the stone bridge where the orange balsam is about to burst into flower. The branched bur-reed was in flower; what a marvellous design; I must it illustrate if time. Common ragwort dots the fields, with the yellow rattle, golden cinquefoil and brown-headed knapweed. Hemp agrimony leans tall over the river, just about to flower, alongside the wild mint. The figwort is already in flower. And to my horror I saw that tiny berries were already forming on the trees and the corn was a ripe sand colour in the distance. Sat down to paint insects before the summer disappears entirely.

July 4th

Murmur of wings as masses of hoverflies collect on the blossom at the bottom of our small garden. Tried to capture them with a paint brush and pencil when suddenly a blue-bottle caught my attention. It really shone in the sunlight, but was evasive; at the slightest movement or shadow it was off, buzzing annoyingly under the flowers and out of sight. I also became aware of some rather stunning green-bottles and tiny worker bees, alongside beetles and slow-moving bumble bees. I was surprised to see so many species of flies feeding on nectar, I tend to associate flies with rubbish tips and carcasses. Other small flies I noticed

[96]

Sketch of a flower & buds
of the plant Comfrey
Symphtum officinale.
Flowers vary from white
to pink, purple and mauve.

1

4

2

3

5

1. Purple Loosestrife. Lythrum salicaria.
Common amongst river bank vegetation
of the Itchen as is Yellow Loosestrife.

2. Hemp Agrimony. Eupatorium
cannabinum. Also common, its
height the same as Loosestrife 1m.

3. Hover fly.

4. Digger Wasp. Ectemnius
quadricinctus.

5. Fly.

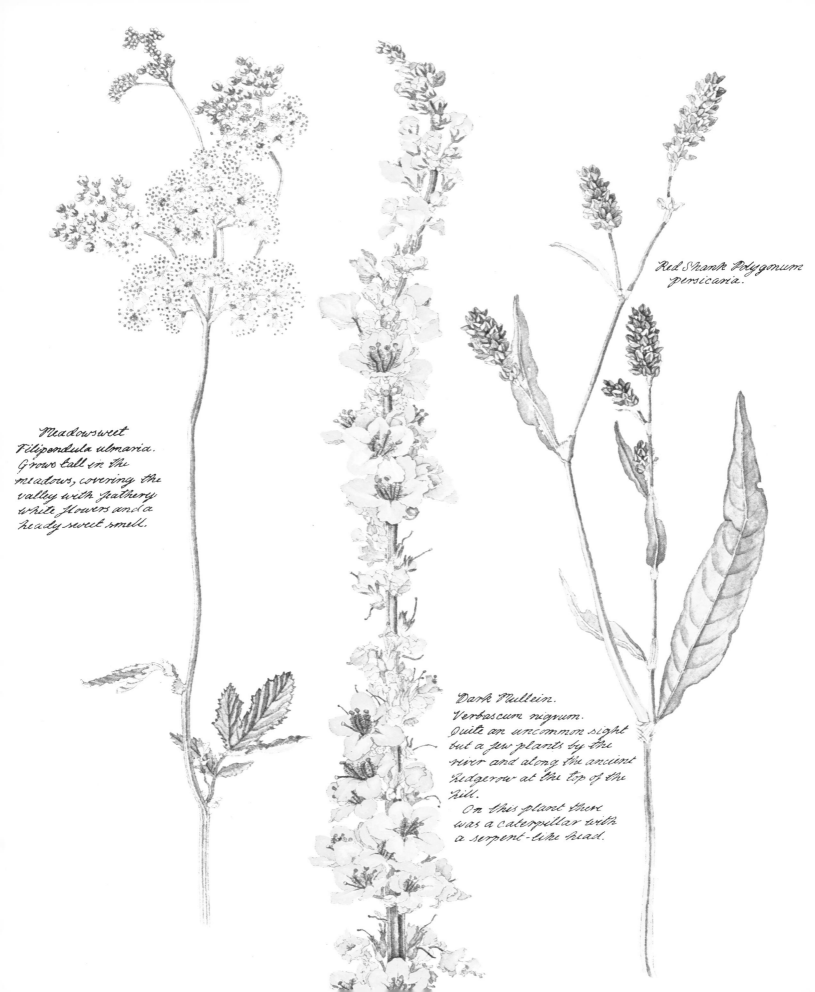

Meadowsweet
Filipendula ulmaria.
Grows tall in the
meadows, covering the
valley with feathery
white flowers and a
heady sweet smell.

Dark Mullein.
Verbascum nigrum.
Quite an uncommon sight
but a few plants by the
river and along the ancient
hedgerow at the top of the
hill.
   On this plant there
was a caterpillar with
a serpent-like head.

Red Shank Polygonum
persicaria.

were predominantly rust-red and all, on close inspection, had quite noticeable hairs on their bodies.

One particular fly, superficially mimicking a bee, sat and looked at me. This fly has been bothering me since very early spring when I saw it on the ivy and wondered what on earth it could eat apart from the nectar of the holly flower. At the time I had been mystified, for this fly looks as though it has been rolling in golden pollen for a week. Tiny specks of gold-yellow cling to its back and legs. I took a photograph of it once while it was sitting on a nettle. I was stung, but the photo came out very well. If I had a dark room I could inexpensively blow it up and produce a clear image of the mystery fly. As it is, I have a mystery negative with a tiny speck of gold centrally placed.

I am always amazed by the variety of flies and their different roles. For instance, never blame a male mosquito for biting you in the night for he feeds quite innocently on nectar and other plant juices; blood-sucking is confined to the female.

Went inside to discover how to identify the less common species of fly in my garden, one of which was a large-winged but delicate fly, with a shape not unlike Concord. I opened a great tome of British Flies, beautifully illustrated. It stated that you must catch your fly, pin it quickly as its bristles break very easily, and then look at the arrangement of bristles above the fly's mouth and eyes to identify it! Easier just to watch both the movement and colour of individual flies as they buzz from flower to flower.

Diverted my attention to the unbelievably tiny and fast-moving worker buff-tailed humble bees. They made the large bumble bees look rather clumsy and heavy in flight. Some bumble bees were yellow overall with pollen dust, their flexible cage or basket bulged with pollen on their hind legs as they returned to the nest. The outer surface of the tibia (leg) is smooth and shiny; but the stout curved hairs on both sides which form the basket area are easily visible. The pollen, picked up by the feathery hairs of the bee's body, is combed off by the front legs, then moistened and passed to the back legs where it is packed away.

[99]

July 5th

The coldest 5th of July for fifteen years, and perhaps the coldest summer for a hundred. I can believe it! Braved the elements and went down to the river to collect a yellow flag to draw at home in comfort. Had a desperate time trying to find a flower that did not look as though it was on its last legs. I noticed that most flowers had a blue or green insect on the petals, much the same colour as the flag's leaves. I picked a flag, and carrying it as carefully as I could managed to retain three of these insects. I had noticed in the past that many of the yellow flag's petals had small holes in them and I think that these insects are the culprits. Having placed the plant in water, I settled down to watching these creatures, which resemble enormous greenfly, as can be seen from my painting.

July 9th

Sat down in the sitting-room with hardboard and paper in hand hoping to get a few hours of work in before the cricket, which I sometimes watch under duress! I had just clipped the paper and paint-box on to the hardboard with an old-fashioned wooden clothes-peg, when my attention was diverted by the chattering of excited sparrows. The grass in the hedge outside had apparently reached edible perfection, or so the sparrows thought. Ten or eleven of these clever little birds were weighing down the heads, now golden in colour, and sharing in a feast with their companions. Their ingenuity has always intrigued me and I watched them for some time. When the sun shines on their feathers they are really quite colourful, although their very abundance seems to stop us taking notice of their plumage and their activities. Sparrows are obviously both clever and adaptable; in the last few weeks I have seen solitary sparrows sitting on the barbed wire near the river, then darting into the air to catch flies.

My attention was drawn to a young thrush under the old-fashioned rose, its head on one side listening intently for worms. The thrush's markings are simply beautiful; the bespeckled chest is covered with pale yellow feathers. This particular bird had what I would call an 'adolescent' beak and a certain impudence and bravado about him. He

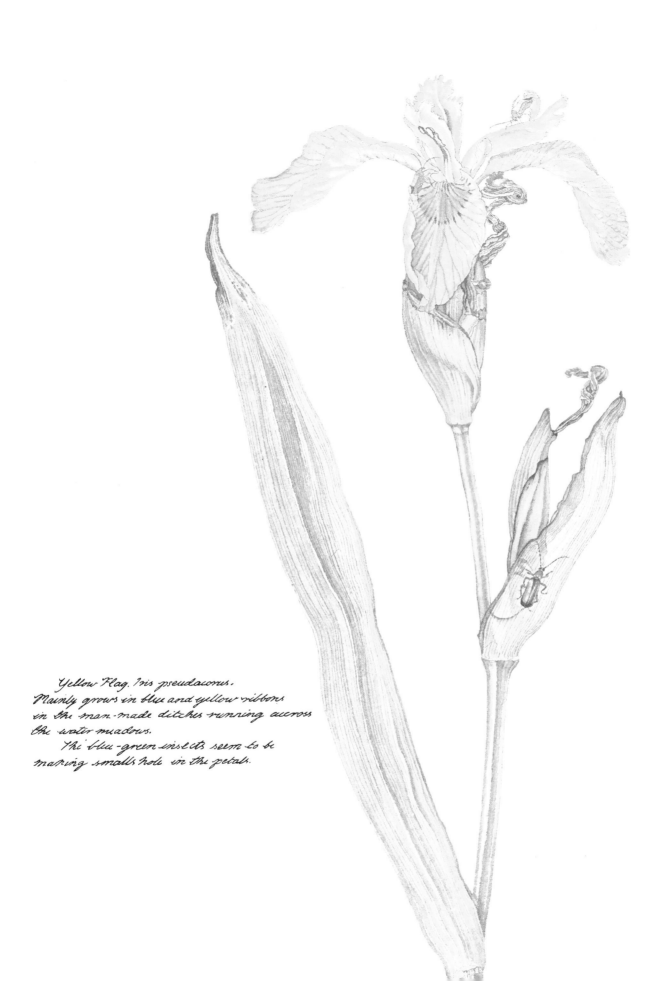

Yellow Flag. Iris pseudacorus.
Mainly grows in blue and yellow ribbons
in the man-made ditches running across
the water meadows.
    The blue-green insects seem to be
making smalls hole in the petals.

cock chaffinch.

was no mean hunter, but as soon as I moved his attention was taken up by me. Bouncing up until just under the window-ledge, he surveyed me at intervals throughout the morning.

Went for a long walk between meadowsweet and thistles and put up two or three young pheasants; or perhaps I should have said 'put down', for they ran like rabbits. However, coming up to one rather makeshift hiding place, I was amused to see that although three-quarters of the young bird was evidently hidden, a rear view of some straggling, scruffy tail feathers was still very much in evidence.

July 10th
I walked down to the river at about seven in the evening, a most beautiful time of day; the water meadows were bathed in warm evening sunshine, adding a richness to the colour of flower and foliage. I paused on the brick bridge to watch the aerobatics of the spotted flycatcher as he took off from the barbed wire, captured flies in mid air and returned, all in the twinkling of an eye. As I watched him, he was joined by a flight of goldfinches, who were interested in the tall mauve thistles in the meadow behind. The red evening light made their plumage all the more brilliant. I followed them to a tree, and to my surprise found that a family of greenfinches were already in residence.

To my left, I saw a slight movement on the trunk of the ash, it was a tree-creeper carefully investigating the bark with his long curved bill. Was there ever a place so rich in bird life? I had not moved a foot and yet had enjoyed seeing so many birds of different forms and habits. In the trees twenty or thirty yards to my left, the chiff-chaff and chaffinch lift up their chorus from their roosting sites.

July 14th
Of the many trials a water-keeper has to face, cattle on his river bank must be high on the list. The banks are fenced off with barbed wire, but a special cattle-drink is left accessible to the animals so that they can go down into the river to drink. Even this area has to be fenced off with wire otherwise the cows would gain access to the banks, and once inside the

[102]

wire the pressure of their hooves in so limited a space does untold damage to the fragile banks.

The cattle come from the New Forest area in the spring. They are young, small but extremely mobile, and some are highly intelligent. One such animal could get through the wire, where he found a loose post, and as easily slip back through it when challenged by authority. This was a great source of annoyance to the water-keeper, but the cow's small size kept damage to a minimum.

Today, when I saw a large cow inside the wire, I realised the situation was potentially serious. It is no easy matter to extricate a cow from the confines of a barbed-wire enclosure and back by the way it came in, without causing great damage to the bank and, more important, to the cow.

While I was trying to make up my mind how to accomplish this, the cow crossed the river and tried to leave it via the cattle-drink. Finding this firmly wired off, she took a deep breath and disappeared under the brick bridge with only her horns showing above the water, like a double periscope. On arriving the other side of the bridge with much snorting, she climbed out of the river, only to find herself confined once more. The situation was now more complicated and I was relieved to see the arrival of the water-keeper.

July 20th
Flowers out on the river bank: great willowherb, purple loosestrife, skullcap, monkey flower, small thistles, hawkweed, black knapweed, hemp agrimony, yellow loosestrife, 'eggs and bacon', and many others.

There was a strong south-west wind and I think the creatures were sheltering from it. The moorhen's nest on the log was empty – I heard that they had all successfully hatched. The wooded area, reeds and meadow were quiet, no calling of young birds and no song – just the alarm call of a cock pheasant and the little cheeping sound of a family of long-tailed tits.

I was sad to see that the domestic-cum-Canada goose was all alone in the field where the other geese usually rest and feed. The goslings are now

Six spot burnet moth.

[103]

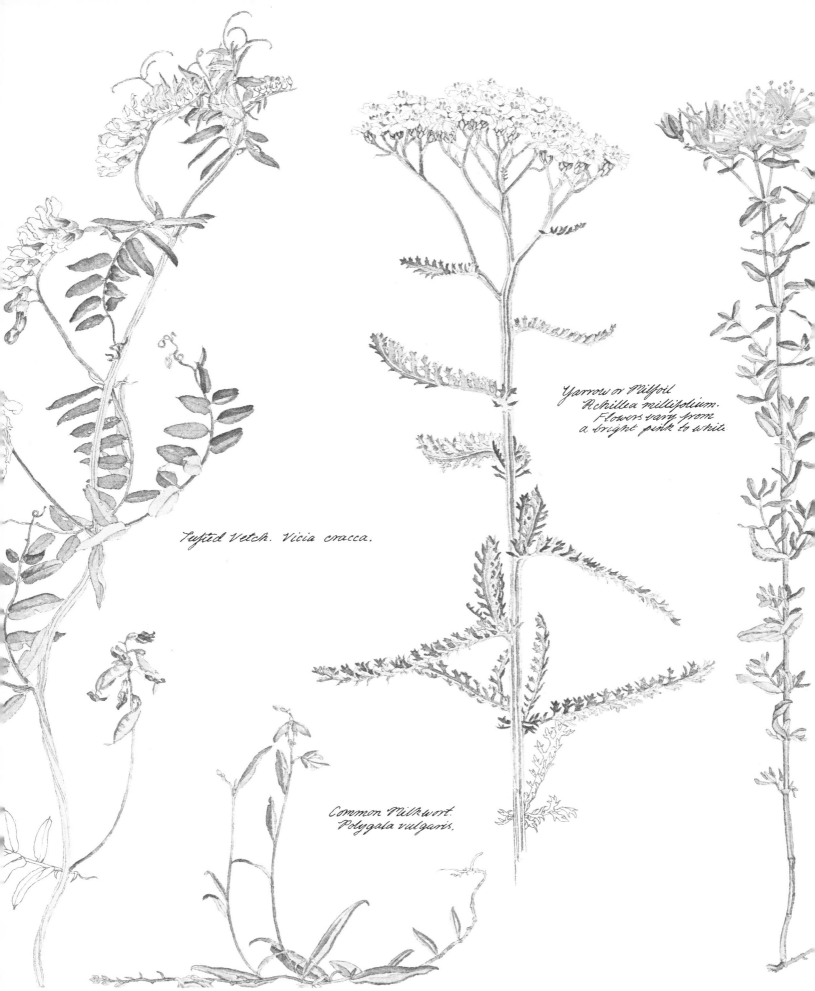

Tufted Vetch. Vicia cracca.

Yarrow or Milfoil
Achillea millifolium.
Flowers vary from
a bright pink to white

Common Milkwort.
Polygala vulgaris.

Buff-tip. Phalera bucephala.
An example of 'broken twig' mimicry.
This particular female was kept overnight
in a jam jar by Mrs Farley in order that I
could draw it.
The eggs she laid
hatched ten days
later.

Spider and her egg sack
woven amongst grasses
and Marsh Bedstraw.

Saint John's Wort
Guttiferae.

Scullcap
Scutellaria
galericulata.
Grows on and
between the tussocks
by the river.

Birdsfoot Trefoil.
Lotus corniculata
Here showing red
buds, the petals
will turn orange and
then yellow as the
flower opens.

Brown Knapweed.
Centaurea jacea.
A beautiful flower,
plentiful in the valley.

Lesser Trefoil. Trifolium dubium.
Covers our drive and creeps into
everybody's vegetable patch.

on the wing and all the Canada geese seem to go off during the day, returning in the early morning for a time. The lonely goose honked every now and again – especially when it heard a duck flying overhead.

That evening I saw eighteen mallard circling the cornfield across the river. They wheeled in ever tighter circles and came lower and lower until I was sure that they were going to land, but they suddenly turned and flew off again.

July 24th

The stoat frequently uses the bridge, which he bounds across in his familiar looping manner. On this occasion I had myself crossed the bridge and walked along the path leading to the carrier. This path is bounded on both sides by tall reeds the height of a man, so I was completely invisible to the stoat. I watched him cross the bridge towards me and wondered what he would do when we came face to face. How close would he approach before he saw me? I had not long to wait. He got within a yard of me, but then had the fright of his life and scampered off into the undergrowth and disappeared.

On another occasion a whole family of stoats accompanied by their parents crossed at the bridge. A fine family of six, and a sight which boded ill for all the young chicks and ducklings.

July 25th

Each time I walk through the water meadows I am reminded of the swiftly-passing summer. In the shafts of sunshine breaking through the clouds, the drifts of sorrel take on a flame-red colour. The fish are now starting to rise to a hatch of blue-winged olives, a species of fly which always hatches as the sun is setting. It has three tails and tall smokey-grey wings. Most other flies have only two tails and hatch earlier in the day. The blue-winged olive has an interesting habit of carrying its eggs in a ball

[106]

clasped to its abdomen. The mature insect has a sherry-coloured body and after releasing its eggs it falls spent on the water; it is known to fishermen as a sherry spinner. Both forms are popular with the trout and both are reproduced as fishing flies.

Later in the evening I saw two young stoats – probably this year's litter. One scurried away at my approach, the other sat on his hind legs to get a better view of me, showing his white front and fine brown coat.

July 30th

I came out of the garden door of the cottage to go down to the river, and I heard the loud droning of bees. The garden was full of them. I watched for a time as a cloud of swarming bees flew about, seemingly aimless, then went on my way. I returned in half an hour to find the swarm had settled on the canary-bird rose bush nearest the sitting-room window. The swarm was about one foot across at its widest, tapering to about six inches. It was about eighteen inches long, domed at the top, straight across at the bottom. Odd bees were joining it and leaving it all the time, but never flying more than a few feet away. I knew of a local bee-keeper and asked him to come as quickly as possible.

The bee-keeper and his son arrived, said the bees looked happy and settled to work. He laid a square of strong white linen on the ground under the swarm, put two small stones on it and rubbed the inside of his home-made skep with the crushed shoot of a broad-bean plant. This, he said, hid any smell that might be in the skep and the bees seemed to like it. He did not know why he used a broad-bean shoot, but his father and grandfather had done so before him. Father and son had been standing close to the rose bush with bees flying round them and even landing on them. It was only when he prepared to put the swarm into the skep that he donned face-netting and gloves. He held the skep in his left hand under the swarm, bent the branch right over and gave it a quick jerk. Most of the swarm fell into the skep, which he quickly turned upside down, with the side nearest the clump of bees on the ground held up slightly by the two stones. The bees clustered round this gap and gradually went inside. Many of the bees had their bodies bent back and their tails in the air;

these were making scent so that other bees from the hive could find the swarm. One bee seemed lost on the edge of the white material and, on picking it up and gazing at its underneath, the bee-keeper declared it to be a young one; it was still hairy-looking. When they are older their hairs get worn away by corn and other rough vegetation they come across in their search for nectar. The life of a bee, in high summer, is about seven weeks.

One bee seemed to be fighting with another. The bee which was getting the worst of it was picked up and immediately flew away; it did not belong to that swarm. Some bees went back to the place where they had swarmed, and this was smoked. A piece of old sacking was burnt in a funnelled can with bellows attached. After a time there were only a few bees flying around; the bee-keeper said there were always a few that did not go in and he did not know why. He then folded the cloth round the skep, tied it round with string, picked it up and went on his way.

He told me that it was not the queen bee who took the swarm away from the old hive, for she would not know where to go. Scout bees go looking for a new home, in roofs or holes in trees, and when they find somewhere they clean it out and then fetch the old queen – the young queen stays behind. I asked him if it was a good thing to take a swarm at this time of year and he quoted the saying:

A swarm in May
    Is worth a load of hay,
A swarm in June
    Is worth a silver spoon,
A swarm in July
    Is worth a butterfly.

He will not get any honey from the bees this year, and they will need feeding through the winter. When they first swarm, as these had just done, they are happy because they are full of honey and well fed.

In time past, to get the honey out of the skep a hole was made underneath it and brimstone fires were lighted which killed the bees.

Honeysuckle or Woodbine.
Lonicera periclymenum.

Bramble. Rubus fruticosus.
Flowers white to pink. The stone bridge
over the "carrier" is covered with bramble
flowers which, in turn are covered with
many hundreds of different insects.

AUGUST

August 1st

A beautiful garden tiger moth was found today by the river and brought up for me to study. It was at this moment that I believe I knew I would become almost entirely involved with insects for at least four or five weeks, and perhaps more. Two years ago my summer sketch books had consisted almost entirely of plants, sheets with scarcely an insect on them. The following year I painted a large picture of water-meadow vegetation which took eleven weeks and into which had crept many animals and insects; the many tiny paintings done in the field of grasshoppers and butterflies followed quite naturally.

The garden tiger moth was large, colourful and inspiring, the colour more subtle than the scarlet tiger moth, which is said to be rare in England, where it is found normally in South Devon and the Channel Islands. However, it invades the valley in great numbers in the heat of the summer sun and is the more common of the two. In 1976 there was suddenly a fantastic hatch of scarlet tiger moths; I drew and painted them in the scorching sun whilst they rested in the shade of the bankside vegetation. It was here that with pencil and paints I captured a rare and rather dreadful sight. A scarlet tiger moth had been caught and was nearly dead in a spider's web, whilst another tiger was trying to mate with this poor struggling insect; try as I would with my paintbrush, I could not get the moth free. The act of courtship is the rarest sight of all and I was very fortunate to have seen it and recorded the moment. I also learnt from that experience that individual tiger moths have slightly different markings.

Unfortunately, I was away for the hatch this year, but I did paint one single straggler on the same page as the garden tiger moth. When these moths sense danger they expose their brightly-coloured hind wings and the garden moth exposes the fringe of red hairs behind the head. The

Mating tiger moths, one caught in a web.

[110]

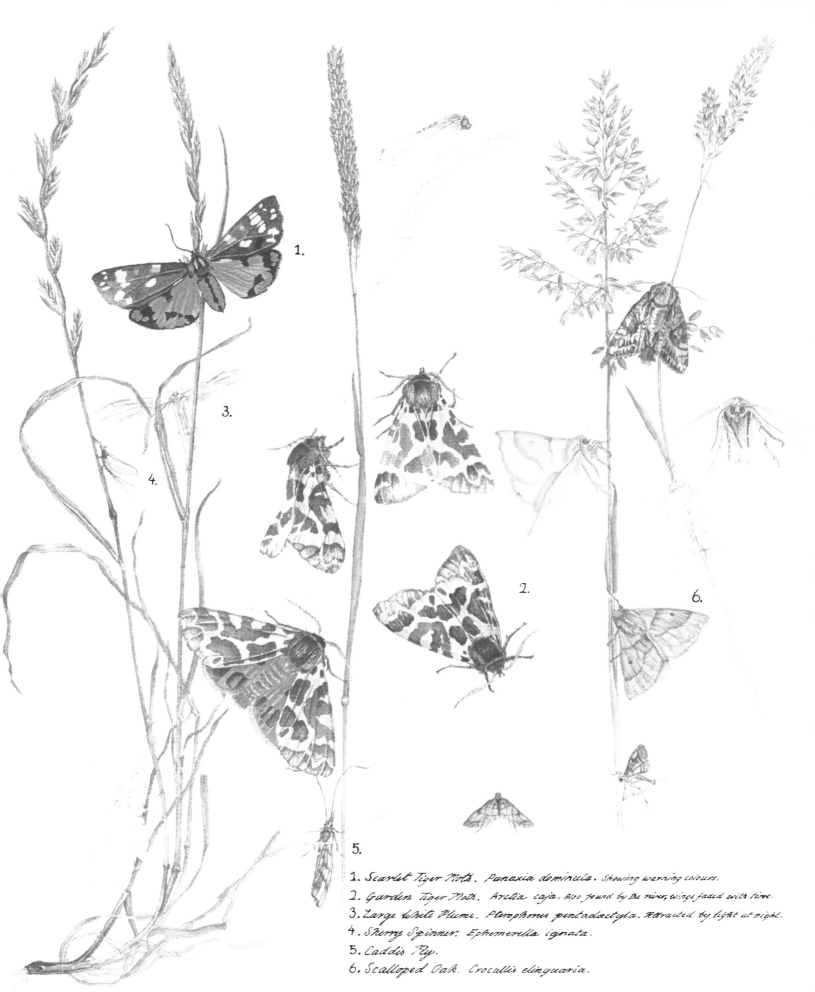

1. Scarlet Tiger Moth. Panaxia dominula. Showing warning colours.
2. Garden Tiger Moth. Arctia caja. Also found by the river, wings faded with time.
3. Large White Plume. Pterophorus pentadactyla. Attracted by light at night.
4. Sherry Spinner. Ephemerella ignata.
5. Caddis Fly.
6. Scalloped Oak. Crocallis elinguaria.

'woolly bear' caterpillars have a partiality for poisonous species of various families of plants, and are capable of extracting toxins from them. These toxins are passed on to the adult moth, which is consequently protected against many predators. Both tiger moths are quite well camouflaged when immobile, but both display hind wings and abdomen when provoked, and also make a small sound, though I have never heard it.

At night, as a protection against the many bats in the Itchen valley, they produce high-frequency pulses of sound associated with inedibility. The sound is produced by the 'tymbal organ', a blister-like part of the thorax which is rythmically distorted.

The tiger moth avoids most predators, but I believe the cuckoo feeds on the 'woolly bear' caterpillar by unzipping the irritant hairy skin and squeezing out the toxins from the caterpillar. They are mysterious and exciting moths, difficult to do justice to with a paint brush and paints.

August 3rd
Found a scalloped oak moth on my window sill this morning; it must have been attracted to the light. Its pale grey eggs, mottled with darker markings, are laid in rows upon many kinds of trees and shrubs. The larvae feed on leaves from September until June, normally hibernating in the winter. The pupae are contained in silken cocoons amongst fallen leaves, rather a hazardous habitat I should think. I have added five sketches of the moth to my page of tiger moths, and intend now to paint some grasses.

Afternoon. Went down to the river, large sketchbook and paints under the arm. Painted in nymph and caddis fly, both amongst bankside grasses.

August 4th
A large white plume moth was captured last night after supper when I saw it through the window. I placed it in a large perspex box. I also saw the triangle plume, which is a rather dull brown, but failed to catch it. The spectacular and magical large white plume is in fact very common, but it is uncommonly difficult to paint. Apparently the hairy larvae feed

white moth.

on bindweeds from August until they hibernate – which they do when still young. In the spring they eat young leaves and flowers, pupating under leaves in May. The caterpillars are green and yellow with long white whiskery spines.

August 5th

I went down to the river alone, feeling sad, for the dog, Fred, has died. He enjoyed sitting by the river watching the life in and around it as much as I did. He suddenly became paralysed and could only lift his head in the end. We all miss him very much.

When walking back from the river, I saw a large number of swallows gathered on the telephone lines; it looked as though they were getting ready to leave very early. It has been such a cold summer that there have been few insects about, and it seems that the swallows have failed to rear their young so they are leaving now. I saw a few swallows and house martins swooping over a field of ripe wheat, just clearing the tops of the grain as they swept by. They also hunted for insects along the roadside hedges.

I watched three sparrows perched on a wire fence at just the right height to reach for ripe grass seeds – they were about two feet from the ground, and were pulling the heads of the grass towards themselves and having a good meal.

The house martins that nest every year under the eaves of the Cricketers' Inn were swirling round and round the old nests this morning, sometimes perching for a short time on the window ledges or wall before dropping off and flying round again. They have successfully reared their young and perhaps now are preparing for their long journey south.

Mrs Farley, my next-door neighbour, found a buff-tip moth last night. She placed it in a large jam jar for me to draw in the morning. It is a beautiful brown moth, a fine example of broken-twig mimicry. I painted the creature and let it go, only to find that on close inspection the jam jar was lined with tiny white eggs. Over the next few days the eggs turned yellow and then dark brown as the caterpillars grew. I moistened them at times with a flower spray and on the tenth day they all hatched, their

black heads and tiny bodies wriggling out of their shells. The caterpillars' favourite food plant is lime, although hawthorn, elm and hazel are acceptable, and I had collected some fresh green lime leaves especially for the occasion, so they did not find it necessary to eat the hard wax-like shells from which they had emerged. I found it surprisingly difficult to remove the egg cases from the glass afterwards. The tiny caterpillars were gregarious to the point of obsession; and, in tightly-packed rows, they ate their way together through one leaf before moving on to the next. I waited for a few days until my tiny caterpillars had grown a little larger and had stripped a few leaves down to gossamer veins, and then, with a couple of leaves and some selotape, I established them all on a large lime to go their separate ways.

1. Eggs. 10 days later. 2. Last one to hatch. 3. Tiny, highly gregarious caterpillars.

The hatching of the buff-tip moth's eggs.

August 6th

A little grebe is nesting once more on a heap of cut weed in the middle of the river. On sighting me, she quickly pulled a large dead poplar leaf and other vegetation over her eggs and slipped into the water.

The young tufted duck are almost fully grown and one can now see which are males and which are females. The drakes are already darker on the back, chest and head than the ducks, and the patches on their sides that will be white are pale grey at present. They are independent now and there are still eight of them; the whole family having survived in spite of the family of stoats.

The river and water-meadow flowers are still lovely: common comfrey, mauve or white, yellow loosestrife just coming out; great willow herb, greater knapweed, figwort, forget-me-nots, meadowsweet, dark mullein and many others. Bindweed in full flower has entwined itself around most of the reeds in the valley.

August 7th

As I sat motionless, I glanced away from the river and saw a hare in the field above the bridge spanning the main river. It too remained quite motionless, and I was able to observe it through glasses. Its long ears were extended to catch the slightest sound and a huge round eye was watching me carefully. We were both aware of each other's presence and I could see the hare's nostrils dilate as he sniffed the air, no doubt alerted by my scent. He remained quite still for several minutes – this beautiful creature so well endowed by nature with the means to get warnings of danger from predators. Then his ears went back and off he went, bounding over the fields.

August 8th

Dusk. Went down to the river with the fishermen and we stopped short at the stile to watch one of the river's most breathtaking sights: a barn owl silently hunting his prey along the river bank. It is an eerie sight; this large white, silent bird following the line of the river, eventually moving out of sight. Later on we heard him calling in the meadows – an alarming sound when the night had gathered in and I was all alone.

It was an unusually beautiful evening; the sky was purple with storm clouds, and the river lay, a ribbon of mauve below us; the meadowsweet and hogweed showed up white against the sky.

I walked along to the main river and marvelled at the height of the nettles – now a full nine feet tall! The marsh orchids were well and truly over, whereas a few weeks ago they had dotted the path in varying shades of mauve. The night was alive with sounds: the water voles near the main river made noisy work of the grasses and weeds of their choice, birds of all species would suddenly call, guarding their territories. Fish sucked noisily at the surface film for tiny nymphs, the water vole swam, hugging the riverbank, and the dry dead reeds cracked as an animal scuttled for safety. And bees still buzzed around the common comfrey although visibility was becoming poor.

I walked rather hurriedly to the seat by the carrier, hoping to catch a glimpse of the owl as he returned from a night's hunting – nothing was

[115]

Studies of blue tits.

to be seen, and as the night grew darker the night sounds became louder and more persistent. Then I heard a loud thud on the bridge behind me. Trying to keep calm and very still, I groped around for a weapon of some kind. A second loud thud followed and I knew it was no small creature that had made it. The hair stood up on the back of my neck as I peered desperately through the ivy fronds. Imagine my relief when I suddenly picked out in the darkness the tips of two long ears. The donkey had been standing silently on the bridge, every now and again kicking out his back against the stone bridge to get rid of unwanted flies.

I was about to return when I saw two familiar shapes coming towards me. The old white goose, named Christmas Dinner, by the water-keeper, and his female friend, the only Canada goose now remaining. I was surprised for I thought these two roosted near the field in which they spent the day lazily cropping the grass. However, they seemed to be making their way to the flighting ponds, probably to remain on the central island sensibly and safely until dawn. I imagined that, like the water vole, their eyes would not be very efficient in the dark and that they would sail right by me if I kept still. This was not so; their eyesight in the dark must be exceptionally good, for they suddenly turned and went upstream in a rather ungainly manner.

I looked at the donkey and, deciding against getting another kick from that animal, I made a large detour, my steps getting more and more hurried until I gained the safety of the cottage.

August 9th
Our next-door neighbour found a caterpillar on her dwarf beans. It was a beautiful black and orange cinnabar moth caterpillar, the black and orange indicating a warning to all predators. It is unpleasant to eat, and birds recognise it and leave it well alone. Its conspicuous larva differs from the rest of the tiger-moth family in being much less furry, although along its back there are short black hairs and at the head and foot of the larva there are long white-grey ones. They hatch from large batches of shiny yellow eggs and feed gregariously and openly in July and August on common ragwort or Oxford ragwort, groundsel and coltsfoot. Our

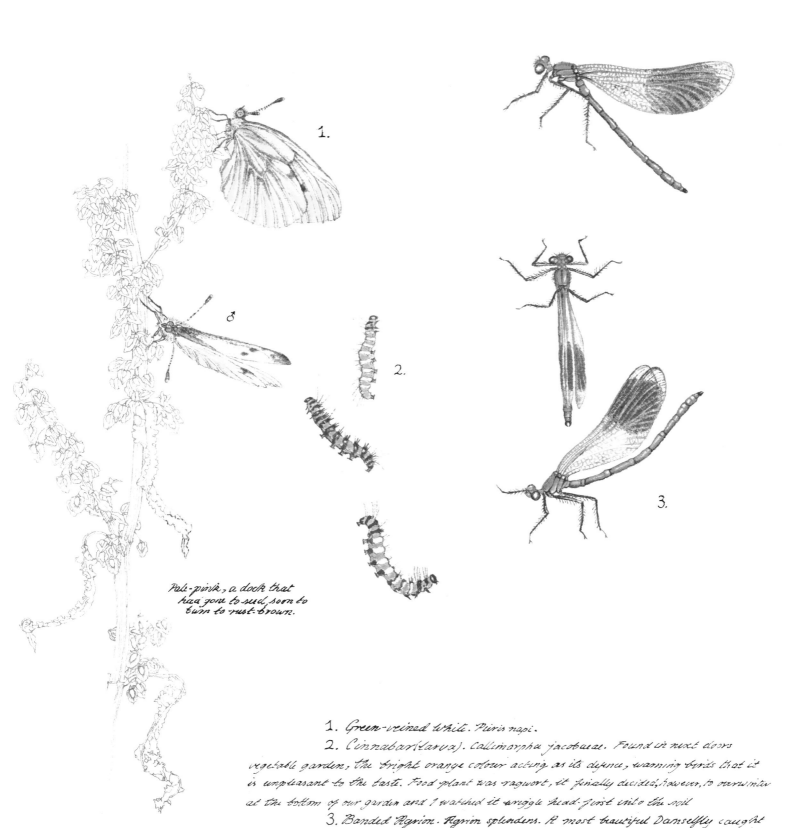

1.

♂

2.

3.

Pale-pink, a dock that
had gone to seed, soon to
turn to rust-brown.

1. Green-veined White. Pieris napi.
2. Cinnabar (larva). Callimorpha jacobaeae. Found in next doors
vegetable garden, the bright orange colour acting as its defence, warning birds that it
is unpleasant to the taste. Food plant was ragwort, it finally decided, however, to overwinter
at the bottom of our garden and I watched it wriggle head-first into the soil
3. Banded Agrion. Agrion splendens. A most beautiful Damselfly caught
for me to draw by a friend and soon set free again to flutter along the river banks.

particular specimen was looking desperately for a spot in which to spend the winter, and finally found one beneath the surface litter at the end of our small lawn. It traversed a great deal of ground quite openly to find this spot and, when worried by passing insects, concertinered itself until quite compact and moved on only when all signs of danger had disappeared. Finally, it burrowed down head first until I could only see its tail, then clasping on to a narrow blade of grass it disappeared from sight to make its thick silken cocoon.

Afternoon. Walked down to the river. The docks had gone to seed, and varied in colour from pale green-pink to sand brown, in some instances a violent dark red. I picked one to draw but when I got home the leaves had wilted and the plant became very dry. On the next sunny day I will go and sit in the field amongst the cows and make colour notes and sketch these docks.

August 10th
I arrived back from London last night to find that Christopher (who is living in the fishing hut and helping the water-keepers) had brought up not only a beautiful and live damselfly for me, but also a dead mole.

He had caught the damselfly by rushing after it with his jacket and finally throwing the jacket over it. Thankfully it was not hurt in anyway, and I was able to place it in a large perspex box and paint it in quite a few positions before releasing it by the river where it was found. It always rests with its wings closed.

August 12th
I was sitting quietly and drawing when alerted by a faint sound of rasping and the crackling of dead leaves. I was astonished to see a wasp on the window sill, desperately tugging at the dry stiff wings of a dead moth. It did not take very long for the wasp to tear away the wings, bit by bit, the dry pieces fluttering on to the ground. The body was then lifted up with some difficulty; the wasp had won its prize. Putting a piece of apple and a morsel of turkey on the sill, I watched for its return. Approximately

[118]

two minutes later a wasp arrived, ignored the apple and took the turkey; it was obviously taking the meat to feed the larvae of its species.

When I'd tired of supplying meat and sketching, I decided that it was time I went to the river. I had recently been given some new and exciting equipment – a collapsible net, some small boxes with transparent lids, and a new lens for my camera. Found a brown tail moth, laying her eggs on the underside of a leaf and carefully collected both leaf and moth to study and draw.

Fruitless but happy times are spent thundering through the water meadows with my wellingtons, two sizes too big, a bikini and old green hat, rushing after an elusive specimen, with camera clutched in both hands. Then suddenly, joy upon joy, the butterfly will settle and you tip-toe breathlessly towards it until it is within range. The moment arrives; but invariably the lens cap is still on, or the film has not been wound on, and the butterfly flutters off. More observations are missed by using a camera than gained by the resulting slides; but when they have been acquired, they do at least bring a breath of summer and a record, if only a haphazard one, of what you were striving for.

On this particular summer day I was cluttered up with equipment for

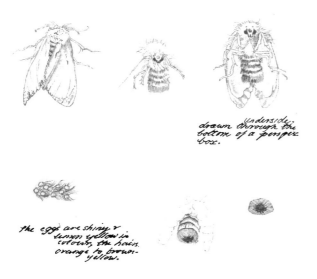

Underside; drawn through the bottom of a perspex box.

the eggs are shiny & lemon yellow in colour, the hairs orange to brown-yellow.

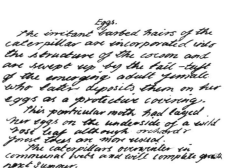

Eggs.
The irritant barbed hairs of the caterpillar are incorporated into the structure of the cocoon and are swept up by the tail-tuft of the emerging adult female who later deposits them on her eggs as a protective covering.
This particular moth had layed her eggs on the underside of a wild rose leaf although orchard & forest trees are more usual.
The caterpillars overwinter in communal webs and will complete growth next summer.

Water meadow plants.
Summer 76.

1 Male common blue butterfly.

2 Leaf beetle.

3 Skullcap

4 Lacewing fly hunting for insects.

5 A toad I found amongst skullcap

6 Creeping Jenny.

7 Underwing of the common blue.

8 Water mint.

9 Yellow loosestrife.

10 Bumble bee. Bombus lucorum.

11 Brookline speedwell.

12 Broad-leaved marsh orchid.

13 Seven-spot ladybird.

14 The common mole.

15 Snail

16 Water speedwell.

17 Chalk stream water crowfoot.

18 Water forgetmenot.

19 Buff-tailed bumble bee.

20 Tiny snail.

21 Froghopper.

22 Male chalk-hill blue butterfly.

23 Seed head of yellow flag iris

24 Yellow flag iris.

25 Bur marigold.

26 The Southern marsh orchid.

27 Watercress.

28 A house mouse.

29 A garden or diadem spider.

30 Lesser scullcap.

31 Small blue beetle.

32 Male and female soldier beetles.

33 Common sorrel.

34 Male orange-tip butterfly.

35 Marsh marigold.

36 Hemp agrimony.

37 Ragged robin.

38 Water avens.

39 Fruit of the marsh marigold.

40 A brown centipede.

fear of missing something. I walked along the familiar lane, past the neat houses with their beautifully-kept small gardens, and past the cabbage field where cabbage whites fluttered amongst row upon row of hand-planted cabbages. Orange ladybirds lined the roadside, sunning themselves on the grass, flowers and docks.

I walked along the path, equipment beginning to be a nuisance, and made a slight detour to the hawthorn where the cows shelter from the rain in winter and the sun in midsummer. I was looking for a small hole I had observed the day before. It had been pouring with rain and, like the cows, I'd run to shelter under the umbrella of hawthorn branches and leaves. To my surprise, a tiny worker bee had scrambled out of a little hole near my left foot and then flown off. Two minutes later a large bumble bee arrived and disappeared down the same tiny hole. The bee was black with a beautiful mid-orange tail.

Determined to take a photograph of bees leaving and rejoining the nest, I put down all other equipment and focused on the hole. Unfortunately, the shutter speed had to be very slow due to shadows from the branches above, and I too was a little slow in getting the best pictures.

Five minutes later, undeterred, I was still standing stock still, my left eye getting tired of being forcibly closed and my ears straining for the faintest buzz, when something ran over my boot. Looking up quickly, I saw the hind legs of a rabbit disappearing into the brambles. How foolish to observe wild life through a camera lens and thereby miss ninety per cent of the natural life around you!

Purple and yellow loosestrife lines the banks of the river, intertwined with bittersweet. The bittersweet is still in flower, but many plants have distinctive and beautiful berries now. The variations of colour are exotic as the berries turn from pale green to yellow and then to red.

The common reed is striking at this time of year, for its nodding head is bright purple, and its stem a fresh green. The branched bur reed is still in flower and I must draw it soon.

Walking towards the main river along the right bank of the carrier, a tiny frog caught my attention. All equipment was flung away as I tried in

[122]

A tiny sub-aquatic plant.

vain to get a better look at the fascinating little creature, but he was in amongst the thick riparian vegetation and, as I brushed the grasses and reeds aside with my hand, I saw him hop on to a small mud bank an inch above water level, then out of sight into the hole of a water vole, conveniently nearby.

August 13th

The hedgerows looked beautiful in the evening light as we wended our way along the ribbon of a road in the direction of the Bush Inn. We always stop to observe the many rabbits in Avington Park, but this evening we witnessed a strange sight in a farmyard. Seeing a family of rabbits we stopped the car, but the mother, only about ten yards away, was too interested in a corn spillage to be alarmed at our approach. Her two young were cropping the short grass that grew where the concrete had cracked. Suddenly the two young rabbits began to gambol like lambs; their powerful hind legs sprung the little balls of excited rabbit into the air again and again.

Cornflowers grew along the hedgerows, the blackberries in some sunny sheltered areas were ripening, and old man's beard was in flower. The countryside looks remarkably lush after all the rain, but the farmers must be worried about the harvest as there have been so few days of sunshine.

On our rather jovial return home from the pub, the barn owl, disturbed by our approach, flew silently off its perch and into the gathering darkness.

August 14th

A most lovely evening. I crossed over the brick bridge and walked up the carrier towards the main river, where I saw a little grebe sitting close into the right bank; she seemed high in the water, but I could not see any nesting material under her. I saw the other grebe diving nearby and, as one bird came close to the other, a tiny black chick appeared from under the mother's back feathers, took food from the father and went quickly back to the safety of mother's body again. So that was why she looked so

moth.

[123]

different from her mate, and that was why she had not dived on seeing me, as they usually do.

August 15th
Sunny, if a little windy. Feeling rather exhausted, I went down to the river, pencil and paint brush in hand. The recent rain storms have made the valley look tatty and unkempt. Some of the thistles were losing their down, and it was surprising how many seeds, looking like tiny silver-spun parachutes, drifted off in the wind from one thistle head. The chaffinches were taking full advantage of the seeds and clung on to the plants tightly as they swayed in the wind. There is quite a high mortality rate on the prickles of thistles. I have found many an over-zealous bee, and quite a few crane flies impaled on the prickles.

I was startled by the colour of the rowan berries; although some were still a yellow-green, most berries which were facing the light were red. The blackberries, though, are still tiny and green.

The male and female brimstone posed for me a number of times. Every year they are to be found in the same territory, usually feeding on thistles, but this year wild mint seemed to be favourite. Probably when the air is still they venture to the thistle heads.

The hogweed by the river was bespeckled with orange, aquamarine green, blue and red insects. Some looked rather sinister with their long and especially adapted ovipositors. The hogweed near the gate on my way down to the river had only harboured rather dull flies and a few two-spot ladybirds.

Found a tiny spider with a big blue ball of eggs inside her cocoon. The size of the spider compared to the enormous ball of offspring always surprises me. There was a great and varied abundance of hoverflies, many with exotic ribbons of colour running round their bodies; they had large compound eyes and tiny strangely positioned antennae.

August 18th
8.10am. Windy, with patches of sunlight piercing the morning mist. The grass was still glistening with dew as I watched a newly-hatched peacock

[124]

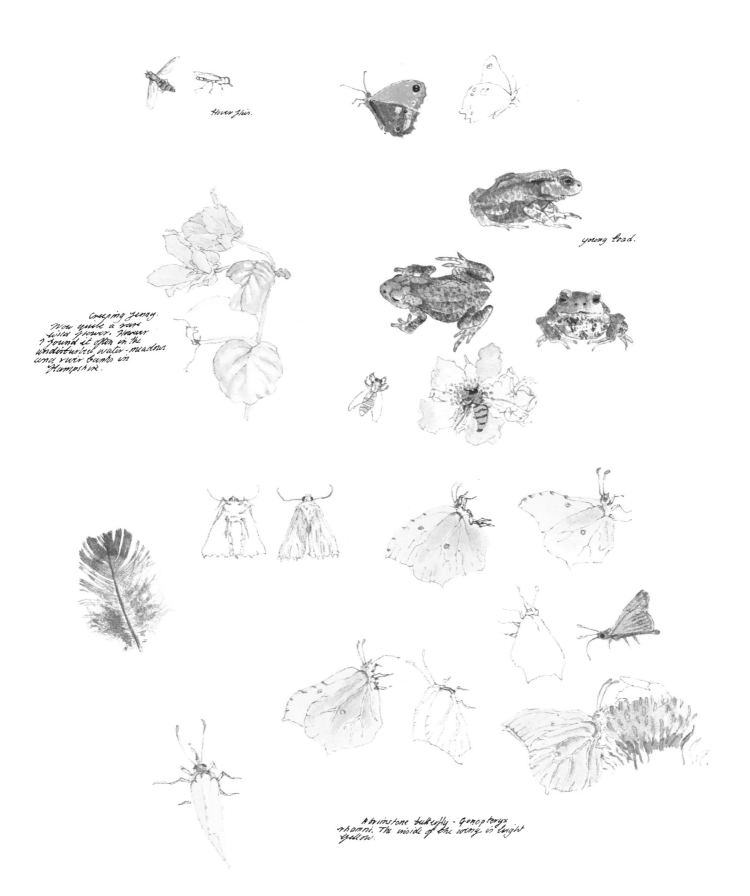

Hover flies.

young toad.

Creeping Jenny.
Now quite a rare
wild flower. However
I found it often in the
undisturbed water-meadows
and river banks in
Hampshire.

A brimstone butterfly - Gonopteryx
rhamni. The inside of the wings is bright
yellow.

butterfly suck nectar from the remaining flowering thistles. Many are already going to seed, their great fluffy heads matted from recent rain. Sure enough, there has been a hatch of peacock butterflies, two or three on every plant; buffeted by the strong wind, their wings were shining in the sun.

I noticed a young blackbird jumping on to a large exposed root of a shrub, fluttering there for a time and then falling off backwards. At first I thought it was trying to get some morsel of food from the far side of the root. The bird did this several times before I realised that it was doing it simply for fun. There were two young birds flying round it in small circles. This was the first time I had ever observed young birds playing as young mammals do.

August 19th

Weather rather dull when we walked down to the river. The hogweed was bespeckled with a small delicate hoverfly, whose wings seemed constantly outstretched, the bands of colour on its almost transparent body varying from orange to yellow. A wasp-like insect shaped like a giant ant drew my attention. Its legs and antennae were yellow and black, the thorax, large head and underside solely black, and the abdomen lemon-yellow with wasp-like black stripes – this creature is, I think, a species of digger wasp. The small metallic-blue beetles have appeared again, seemingly having had many hatches through the summer. Other small insects wandered around with long antennae, their ovipositors sticking into the air whilst they collected nectar. I believe that these particular insects are parasitic on the goat moth; they are common in this area. Their larvae can be seen in the autumn and they have a repulsive, goat-like smell. The ovipositor, about a quarter of an inch long, is necessary to reach the host larvae, which bore long tunnels into the solid wood and take three or four years to become fully grown.

Shieldbugs seem to be less in evidence this year; grasshoppers, however, 'sang' by the river in great numbers and jumped this way and that, sometimes flying to safety as I walked by.

[126]

shieldbug

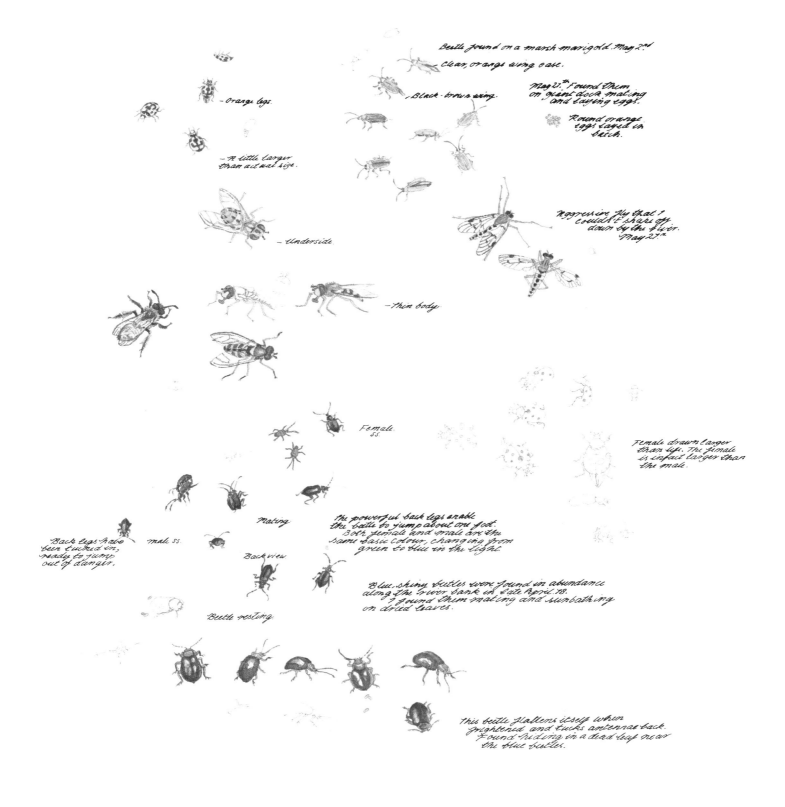

Beetle found on a marsh marigold. May 2nd

Clear, orange wing case.

- Orange legs.

Black-brown wing.

May 21th. Found them on giant dock, mating and laying eggs.

Round orange eggs layed in batch.

- A little larger than actual size.

- Underside.

Aggressive fly that I couldn't shake off down by the river. May 27th.

- Thin body.

Female. ss.

Female drawn larger than life. The female is infact larger than the male.

Mating

Male ss.

Back legs have been tucked in, ready to jump out of danger.

The powerful back legs enable the beetle to jump about one foot. Both female and male are the same basic colour, changing from green to blue in the light.

Back view

Blue, shiny beetles were found in abundance along the river bank in late April 18. I found them mating and sunbathing on dried leaves.

Beetle resting.

This beetle flattens itself when frightened and tucks antennae back. Found hiding in a dead leaf near the blue beetles.

Eating
geraniums in
February.

Tiny white
spots.

Stick-caterpillar
eating.

Orange balsam dangled its snapdragon-like flowers over the now sunlit surface of the water. The thistledown had a tousled, rained-on look.

The water-keeper had rather overdone the cutting back of the riparian vegetation at the water's edge and so one had to struggle through the reed beds to find yellow loosestrife in full flower. The reeds themselves were about eleven foot tall, all with purple plumes that shone in the sun. Peacock butterflies, making black shapes when their wings are folded, fed on the few surviving thistle flowers. The brimstones were near the bridge again, the sun shining through their colourful wings.

The small skipper butterfly fluttered everywhere; they are a beautiful orange-brown in colour, but have rather primitive, moth-like stout bodies. They seem to hold their hind wings horizontally, the forewings tilted at an angle of forty-five degrees. The males have a black line on their forewings, which is a streak of scent scales.

I sat very still, listening to the grasshoppers, and to a water vole's noisy eating habits. I picked a lot of watercress and went up to the cottage to make some delicious soup.

3.30pm. Saw a linnet in its autumn plumage whilst writing today's news. I was prompted to go outside again and study the wild life in our tiny vegetable patch. Most of the red cabbages looked like lace work, having taken the full brunt of the insect attack so far. I had a look at a couple of caterpillars living at the base of the cabbage leaves. One was rather a dull brown with darker markings on its head, the other a beautiful emerald green; I could have sworn that these same caterpillars had been wintering in my London geraniums; perhaps they were not very choosy about their food plant. I inspected the underside of the green cabbage leaves and they were covered with yellow conical-shaped cabbage white butterfly's eggs. I have watched them being laid singly and with care by the female butterfly over the weeks, her abdomen curving upwards to deposit a rather pale egg on the underside of the leaf. The eggs become a deep shade of yellow when the egg is about to hatch. The slugs seem to have enjoyed the lettuces, which are now useless and going to seed to boot; and the sparrows have tucked into the spinach and the

[128]

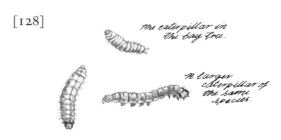

The caterpillar in
the bay tree.

A larger
caterpillar of
the same
species.

blackfly are coping quite well with the beans – both a gourmet's and gardener's nightmare, but at least it's a nature reserve.

August 20th
At last a beautiful summer morning with the promise of a hot day to follow. As I was approaching the river, I saw a heron flying quite low over the water with slow beats of its great broad wings. It soon saw me and made off, emitting a harsh cry which expressed what it thought about fishermen, and water-keepers in particular.

Walking along the banks once again, I found a large decapitated eel, but this time with its tail intact. Again, this is the work of the otter, who does not chew the meat down the backbone, as the mink does, but eats only the head and tail.

August 21st
Today I saw one of the little grebes sitting on a heaped portion of a raft of old cut weed. It was not her original nest and was at the side of a little 'harbour' of still water in the weed raft. She must have pulled weed up to make a resting-place for her family. One of the adult birds was diving and feeding some way off. Then the sitting bird left the weed, leaving three tiny chicks on the platform. They got into a sheltered patch of water and swam about. The young, which are not black but dark brown when seen closer, came and went from the water on to the nest, and the adult birds began feeding them. They must have been feeding them with something very small for I could not see what it was. The young have orange beaks, not quite as bright as a cock blackbird's,

I came nearer. After some tiny, brief alarm sounds the hen bird joined her chicks and swam away, with three young behind her, swimming hard to catch up. They were soon safely on board amongst her feathers, and she swam to the bank and sat still amongst the roots of the herbage.

The blue tits and chaffinches have lost their bright colours and are looking drab and bedraggled. They have had a hard summer, flying many miles a day to feed their young. Now they are moulting and have ceased to sing, for there is no longer a need to claim a nesting territory.

Black caterpillar flecked with white and yellow

Brown —

[129]

n species of wood louse.

— Discarded skin from head and body from growing black caterpillar.

A wall butterfly found on Farley Mount.

August 22nd

At last I am able to enjoy a fine summer evening sitting on one of the wooden benches overlooking the main river. In the distance the combine harvester works to and fro reaping the corn. The monotonous noise has an almost hypnotic effect, as gradually the area of standing corn diminishes and stubble appears in its place. Presently I am joined by the water-keeper. We talked of the great agricultural revolution which had taken place in his lifetime. He recalled that as many as thirty mowers used to reap a field of this size. They must have been a fine sight, sweeping their great scythes in unison.

As we were talking, a brace of hares bolted from the field, pursued noisily by an excited cocker spaniel, who was quickly outdistanced.

Near to us was a grey wagtail, collecting flies, with rapid little rushes to and fro. We admired the brilliant yellow patch under his tail and his dexterity as he darted here and there flicking his tail up and down all the while. He appeared to be a mature bird and I wondered what had become of the chick which I had seen being fed by his parents earlier in the year.

August 23rd

7.30am. Visited Farley Mount. I had forgotten my boots, which was a pity as it was bitterly cold and wet underfoot. The sun was desperately trying to pierce the mist, and it was obvious that eventually it would be a fine sunny day.

Not a bee buzzed as yet so I would have the pleasure of watching the insect world awaken. The plants are thrilling on Farley Mount: wild thyme, with its pink flowers, grows everywhere and smells marvellous at this time in the morning. In amongst the thyme nod the blue-mauve heads of scabious, and the delicate hairbells shiver on their slender stems in the early morning breeze. A predominantly blue papery flower grows everywhere in the short grass, its flowers sometimes the palest of pink. Cloudberries ripen underfoot; I remember when I first saw this species thinking that it was just a small undernourished blackberry bush, but I was baffled by the berries which had few segments and the most stunning blue bloom on them. However, they taste almost the same as any

Eyebright. Euphrasia offinalis.
Divided into many species
but very difficult to distinguish
them.

Wild Basil. Clinopodium vulgare.
Both basil and wild thyme
smell wonderful in the early
morning when crushed underfoot.

Bedstraw. Family - Rubiaceae.

Fragrant
Orchid.
Gymnadenia
cmopsea.

Yellow Rattle. Rhinanthus minor.
Also common by the river, the
seed pods, when brown and dry,
rattle in the wind.
Especially common near the
caravan by the 'carrier.

Common Wild Thyme.
Thymus praecox.
This plant covers the hill, its
scent and taste is much milder
than the garden variety.
Many shrubs are quite large.

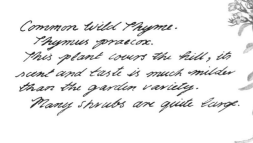

Autumn Gentian.
Gentianella amarella.

Harebell.
Campanula
rotundifolia.

blackberry. I must paint them before the summer draws to a close.

The sun was making some headway now and the view was staggering from the top of the hill; I was able to see past the acres of forest over many cornfields, and many miles beyond, the distant blueish form of the downs.

Putting down a hand to a perfect scabious flower, I was surprised to find a bee on its underside; it slowly lifted one back leg to protect itself, obviously being about as awake as I was. I withdrew to the car with a handful of cloudberries and a few tiny plants to draw during the day.

August 25th

I went down to the river at 3.00pm with the two children and friend who are staying, and their dog, Toby. We had two little nets, a butterfly net, jam jar and binoculars. No sketchbook today, weather windy and wet with sunny patches. Yesterday's torrential rain had flattened almost all of the riverside plants. However, I found a huge and beautiful black slug on the path. He had formed himself into a ball for protection, and as I had no notebook or paints I put him in a leaf-lined box and took him up to the house to draw.

I waded into the river with my boots on and found something of interest for the children – a small caddis fly larva, in a reed case.

August 26th

Very hot and windy. At 12.15pm I walked down to the river in order to draw some orange balsam and bittersweet. Took a photo of a small toad which, surprisingly enough, had only one back leg, and I found some small frogs.

Saw both male and female brimstones. The female is greenish-white, not unlike the cabbage white butterfly, but with a stronger and more direct flight pattern. I saw the following butterflies: large white, green-veined white, small white, red admiral, peacock (which I think flies like a bird, using the wind to sail swiftly along), small tortoiseshell, small heath, meadow brown, and a comma. I was thrilled with the comma, caught it carefully in my net and took it back to draw, paint and observe, then finally set it free.

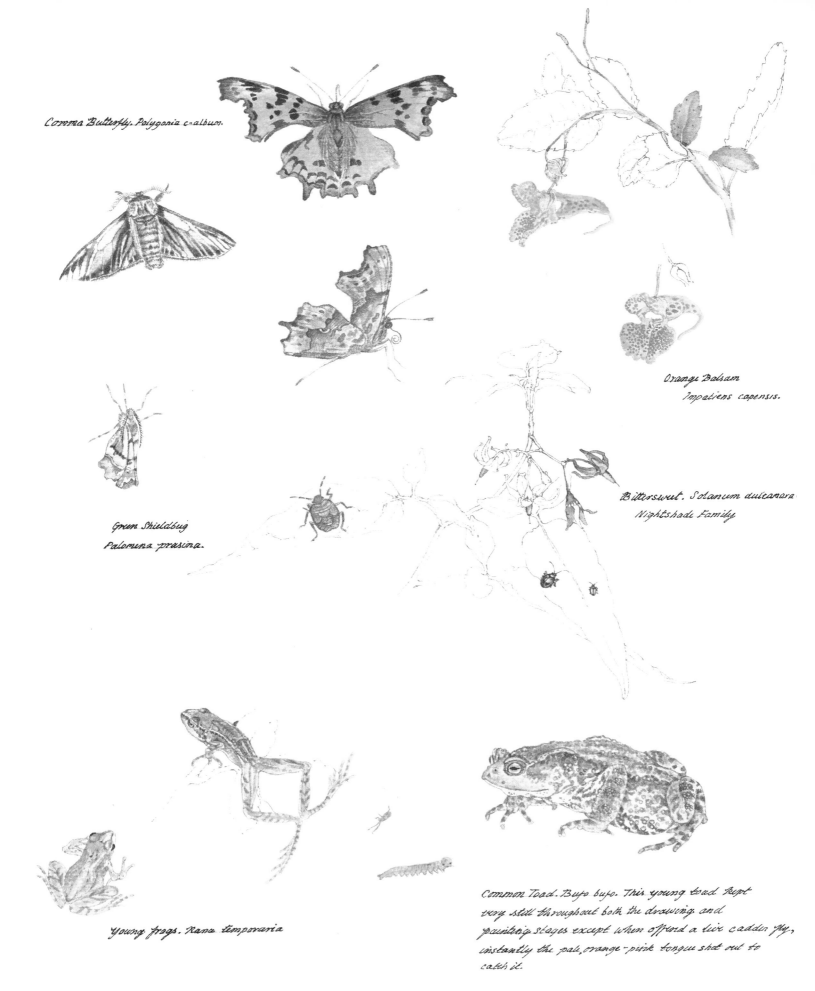

Comma Butterfly. Polygonia c-album.

Orange Balsam
Impatiens capensis.

Green Shieldbug
Palomena prasina.

Bittersweet. Solanum dulcamara
Nightshade Family

Young frogs. Rana temporaria

Common Toad. Bufo bufo. This young toad kept
very still throughout both the drawing and
painting stages except when offered a live caddis fly,
instantly the pale, orange-pink tongue shot out to
catch it.

Dragonfly. The Common Aeshna. Aeshna juncea. Found by the road Sept.

SEPTEMBER

September 3rd
It has been a day of continuous fine rain, but quite warm. In the evening
the heavy clouds parted, and as I walked down towards the river, shafts of
intense golden light picked out flowers and foliage. Suddenly I came upon
a sight which halted me in my tracks. One of these shafts of warm evening
sunlight had brilliantly illuminated a peacock butterfly, which had
settled for a few moments on a flower. It was a thing of delicacy and
quivering beauty, and I can see the beautiful little creature yet, although
in an instant it was gone into the shadows and the image was shattered.

September 6th
I saw a female kestrel, with feathers a chestnut brown and banded from
head to tail, perched on a branch near the river. The male has a blue-grey
head and tail with a black band at the end. The plumage of the sparrow
hawk is much darker; slate grey for the male and grey-brown for the
female, rather than the warm rufus brown of the kestrel.

September 17th
The Canada geese were feeding on the burnt stubble where, but a few
weeks ago, the combine harvester was working. The flock is now as large
as sixteen pairs, with the goslings in their adult plumage. Each night with
much noisy honking they take off in groups of twelve and fly over the
river to spend the night in one of Mr Gray's fields. Christmas Dinner flew
with them bravely enough, but was soon seen to be losing height and was
obliged to make a forced landing this side of the river. The others flew
onwards, leaving him to await their return.

September 18th
Went to Farley Mount to see if I could find some fungi to paint. It was too

dry, but I saw some exciting things while searching for them. On gently pulling two leaves apart, I saw a spider's egg sac; a ball of cobweb, with tiny spiders inside it ready to emerge. The mother was there, a small pale green spider; perhaps she was going to open the sac so that the young might get out. Some female spiders produce a sort of a pulp for their young to feed on when they leave the egg sac.

It was a lovely autumn day with a fresh wind, but warm in sheltered places. Many creatures seemed to be sunbathing. I had a brief glimpse of a lizard, and saw a large pale brown cricket; he must have been about 45–55mm long, but he was not green, and was just the colour of the dead leaves around him.

I saw a dead hoverfly hanging from some grass seeds. Looking closer, I found that it was being held by a round white spider of its own size. The fly had just been caught, it had web about it. As I peered at it the spider fell to the ground leaving the fly behind. There were many brown bespeckled butterflies about, some sunning themselves and

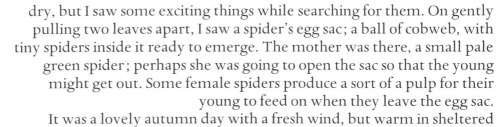

others feeding on hemp agrimony.

Thwarted in my attempt to find
fungi, however, I have decided to insert a
painting that I have been working on during
weekends in Sussex. The richness of fungi life in Sussex
compared to that in Hampshire is unbelievable. The
painting, although out of context, shows the beauty and
variations of the fungi form.

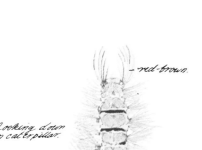

Head & legs.

brown eyes—

Brownish hairs behind head give fringe impression.

Underside - jet black.

Defence.

— red-brown.

Looking down on caterpillar.

PALE TUSSOCK.
Also known as HOP DOG.
Larvae feed on a number of trees,
chiefly elm, oak, birch and hazel. Also
eats hops and the leaves of fruit trees.

September 19th

Got up at 7.00am. A watery sun did its best to pierce the thick valley mist. I walked sleepily down to the river with my camera, turning left across the stile to walk along the bank. It was unbelievably cold, and the long vegetation whipped across my knees and jersey; my knees became soaked with dew, whilst my jersey sparkled like the countless spider webs around me. Many cobwebs hung heavy with dew, along the barbed wire, while patches of web of different sizes made a small hawthorn glisten. Many cobwebs sagged and broke under the strain as the sun grew warmer. I became carried away by these diamond-studded designs, only to find that my camera had but one frame left. I went back to the cottage, searching for another film but found none. On returning, I climbed the massive broken willow, at the parting of the ways of carrier and main river, to watch the mist slowly disperse. It is at moments like this, totally at peace in a silent white glistening world, that I am truly happy.

September 26th

Today, whilst walking by the river, I saw a good-sized pike lying motionless in a bay, surrounded by water celery. As I watched, the pike began to drift 'stern' first with the current. At first I thought it was quietly making its escape, but it made no effort to swim, and continued to drift backwards with the stream. Presently it drifted opposite a trout of about one pound, and pounced like lightning, grabbing the trout in its jaws. It was able to swim with difficulty, crab-wise across the river with its victim, which it no doubt took to its hole and devoured.

Rowan or Mountain Ash, plentiful by the river.

OCTOBER

October 2nd

Walked to my favourite hedgerow to find spindle berries, or anything else that truly catches the eye, for the cover of my book. But sadly, half the ancient hedgerow has been literally ripped asunder by a mechanical cutter. A quarter of the older yew has been destroyed, and the oldest and finest spindle tree has been cracked in half. There is now room not only for one tractor, but three abreast. It seems to me a destructive move, and no doubt it will be slashed yearly by the farmer. I made an inward note to find out the name and whereabouts of the farmer and to write a short letter of grievance.

Gained a sprig of spindle berries by climbing up the tree, but as yet the fruit has not split to reveal the bright orange seed.

October 5th

Went to investigate the vegetable (or should I say wildlife) plot at the bottom of the garden. The sweet peas were flowering beautifully, the beans were nearly over and many of the cabbages had already been stripped bare, leaving the stem and a few ribs of cabbage branching outwards. One could trace the caterpillar's history on each plant. First, the leaf had been eaten by the tiny newly-hatched caterpillars, leaving a skeleton as fine as gossamer behind them. Stuck to this gossamer were their shrivelled-up discarded skins, covered with tiny hairs all about one eighth of an inch long. They are gregarious creatures, even now that most of them are quite large, a cluster of yellow and black bodies lying across one another as they eat. This may, of course, be because there are so many caterpillars and not enough plants! These are the caterpillars of the large white butterfly and they predominate; however, intermingled are one or two caterpillars of the small cabbage white; pale, blue-green in colour with a yellow streak on their sides. They, along with an ugly brown caterpillar, seem to prefer the red cabbage to the broccoli. The foodstuff dictates the colour of droppings; the droppings on the red cabbage, and there are a great quantity of them, are all an exotic pink; they also seem to be destroying the heart of the cabbage by becoming mouldy and mildewed. I bent an ear to listen to what I thought would be audible cabbage-crunching by masses of caterpillars, but I straightened up rather quickly, for the keen gardener next door was watching my antics with puzzled interest. I looked at the cabbages sadly, and remembered the day when I most carefully removed, with the aid of a spoon and cardboard box, all the small cabbage-white caterpillars to re-settle them on a plant removed from the main crop. It took me hours and was quite obviously a futile exercise.

October 7th

The foliage of the plants by the river is colouring, making it easy to pick out the species at a distance. A few weeks ago all were merged into one homogeneous mass of green, but now each species colours at the same time and is picked out as though by some kind of natural *son et lumière* effect.

The fruits are also well advanced and one can see, in addition to the scarlet berries of the guelder rose, the crimson fruits of the spindle tree, the berries of the hawthorn and the jet-black berries of the wild privet and elderberry. Dog rose hips are to be found amongst the ripening blackberries.

The birds are now gathering into great flocks. The Canada geese are now as many as 70-80 head, and the peewits twice that number. Flocks of starlings gather noisily in the trees, and the house martins in numbers are assembling on the telephone wires, looking rather like the notes in a musical score. Their departure appears to have been delayed by a prolific hatch of insects in the warm weather.

The aquatic flies are hatching on the river, mainly around midday, but the blue-winged olives still hatch in the evening.

The spinners are now to be seen flying by the river at midday. In mid summer they only made their appearance at dusk. These adult flies are

[141]

Snail - now in hibernation
behind a peat bag.

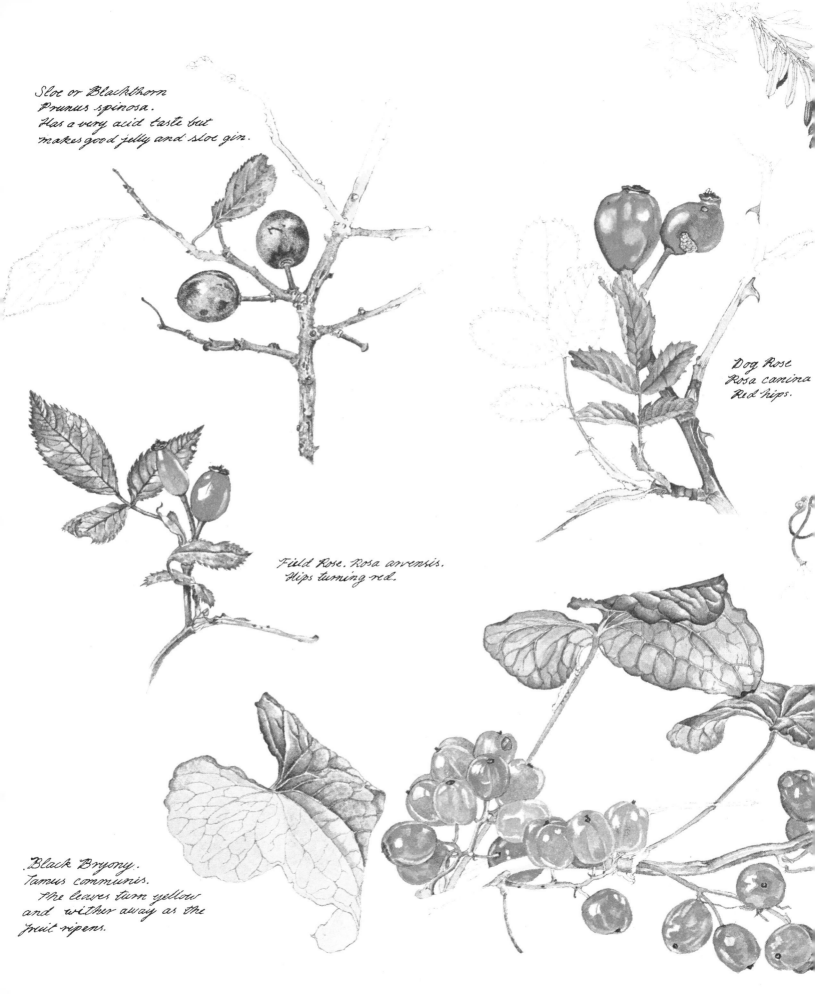

Sloe or Blackthorn
Prunus spinosa.
Has a very acid taste but
makes good jelly and sloe gin.

Dog Rose
Rosa canina
Red hips.

Field Rose. Rosa arvensis.
Hips turning red.

Black Bryony.
Tamus communis.
The leaves turn yellow
and wither away as the
fruit ripens.

Fruits of the Ancient Hedgerow at the top of the Hill, Easton

Yew. Taxus baccata.
   Here showing the red
   fruit and leaves.

Spindle-tree. Euonymus europaeus
   Has brilliant orange seeds, a favourite
   of blackbirds.

Traveller's Joy or Old Man's Beard.
Clematis vitalba. The ripe fruits with their
silvery long awns. Drapes shrubs and the
tallest trees in October.

A golden body with bright red, compound eyes.

beautiful little creatures, with clear transparent wings and long tails. In this, the final stage of their existence, they are unable either to eat or drink, their sole object being to mate and lay their eggs.

The male flies congregate over the river and its immediate neighbourhood, rising and falling as if performing a nuptial dance. The female flies into this throng, mates with one of the males and later lays her eggs in the river. The females of the Bactis family of flies descend under the water to lay their eggs, often on some submerged structure such as the piers of a bridge.

October 15th
The weather is still dull and misty, but not so warm and I fear we may have a change. The fish rose occasionally to a hatch of pale wateries and the grey wagtail was just as active, searching for flies on the rafts of weed.

Where the carrier joins the main river was a pair of dabchicks. First one would dive under the water and then the other. Sometimes when they met they greeted each other with their peculiar winnowing call.

Returning along the carrier, I saw the kingfisher flash by once again. This time it was above me, for I saw only the beautiful chestnut of its underside and none of the green of his back. I have seen kingfishers so many times on the river but unfortunately I have never discovered the hole in the bank where they nest.

On one occasion I was entertained by watching it fish. It would perch about three or four feet above some shallows and dive into the water, and as often as not it would emerge with a small fish in its bill. The fish was first killed by being hit on a stone and then quickly swallowed. The operation is a learnt procedure and the young kingfisher takes some time to become proficient. In the process of learning, it gets rather wet and bedraggled.

Autumn is now well advanced. The day started cool and misty but the sunshine soon broke through. The river is clear as glass, looking quite shallow, and the water weeds are luxuriant. The long tresses of ranunculus move gently in the current. The autumn colours of the

Looking through glass at the underside.

Small brown dots on either side of stripe

Lacewing - soft emerald green with bright yellow stripe running down body.

underside

Brown-red eyes as opposed to the red of the golden lacewing.

foliage are caught by reflections in the stream; in particular the dark red berries of the guelder rose.

October 16th
While sitting by the main river watching the fisherman creeping up on a rising fish, I heard and saw the Canada geese arriving in the field – which has now been ploughed and shows a film of green. There were ten of them and they seemed to rest before starting to feed on the wheat which was growing in the adjoining field. Christmas Dinner and his Canadian companion were in the corner of the river beside the grass meadow, between the river and the ploughed field. They heard the geese arrive and they both got out of the water and walked towards the gaggle of geese; the hybrid goose soon stopped, but the other went on calling to them. Then she stopped, stood still for a while and went back to her companion and they both returned to the river.

   Just before I reached the carrier this morning, I heard a sudden loud raucous noise coming from behind the white poplar trees. I thought at first that a stoat was killing something, but it continued too long and was too loud. I went along the riverbank by the trees and saw jays flying amongst the may and willow bushes; in a little while the raucous noise ceased and I counted ten as they flew away. I had only seen solitary jays before and wondered why they had gathered and why they had made so much noise.

October 22nd
Went down to the river with the fishermen in the morning taking a picnic basket, as it was a still, beautiful day.

   On reaching the main river and walking towards the chestnut tree, I saw a lone mallard duck sitting on some boards at the edge of the bank. I had seen her by herself the day before and wondered why she was not with the rest of her kind in the area of little streams and marshland behind the carrier where the mallard live most of the year. She seemed to be enjoying the warm sunshine; as the fishermen moved down towards her she slipped into the water, and a few yards further down was

[145]

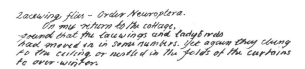

Lacewing flies - Order Neuroptera.
   On my return to the cottage,
found that the lacewings and ladybirds
had moved in in some numbers. Yet again they clung
to the ceiling or nestled in the folds of the curtains
to over-winter.

Flight seems
slow and
hazardous.

joined by one small duckling. The duckling was still very young, nowhere near ready to fend for himself.

I sat on the seat by the sleeper bridge and the huge golden-leafed

Adult coot.

Coot chicks.

Coot young, have white throats.

Mallard duck. ♀

Mallard young.

♂

Mallard-drake.

chestnut tree and looked up river. Two swans were feeding. Soon I
noticed that they had ceased to feed and were displaying; each bird
stretched its neck upwards, then curved it and placed its head under the
water for a second before repeating the performance. Sometimes they
were near to one another, sometimes further apart, often they were in
unison. After about ten minutes they added the rubbing of their sides
with their beaks and heads to the first sequence of movements, this part
of the ritual coming after immersing their heads in the river. After about
another ten minutes, they were going through the sequence of head and
neck stretching, curving the neck, head in the water, and rubbing their
sides with their heads, faster and faster till finally they were touching one
another. Then the cob put his neck over the pen's when immersing his
head, and shortly after that he mounted her. They stood right up in the
water facing each other, rubbing heads; it was intriguing to see how much
interest they showed in one another after mating; many birds seem to
part immediately afterwards. Swans, it seems, mate for life. Although it
was warm and sunny it was not spring, and I wondered why they were
mating in the middle of October. I learnt later that this was bonding
behaviour. They moult in July, August and September.

I was pleased to see that the hybrid goose was no longer alone – its
Canadian friend was with it again. But there was no sign of the other
Canada geese. I do not know where they have gone. Apparently the pair
of swans I watched this morning called the large hybrid goose yesterday
and it joined them on the river.

At dusk, one of the fishermen saw a new arrival – a hybrid duck –
competing with the trout for flies when masses were hatching. The trout
were not bothering to go back to their lies after each fly, but were
cruising on the surface of the water collecting them, and the duck was
darting about snapping flies up just as the fish were about to eat them. I
found the duck, which was predominantly white, dead on the riverbank
a few days later.

The fruit of the ivy is as
yet unripe, late October.
Notice the shape of
the leaves as compared to
the non-flowering stem.

Ivy. Hedera helix.
Common by the river on the
ground and up to the tallest
branches.
   This is a non-flowering,
climbing stem I found amongst
the mosses. The flowering shoots
have long thin leaves, see
illustrations of ripening fruit.

NOVEMBER

November 1st

I found a strange long black beetle walking on the carpet. It seemed to have many joints and was over an inch long. When I picked it up it curved its hind body over its back and held its mandibles wide apart and snapped fiercely. I looked it up in my insect book and found it was a devil's coach horse. When it senses danger it apparently lets out a nasty smell as well, but fortunately I hadn't suffered this. I kept it in a jam jar for a while, feeding it on tiny scraps of meat and apple and spraying it with water from time to time. The meat was devoured rapidly and the liquid licked from sides of the jar. I did not get round to painting the creature as I had intended to so I took him into the garden and let him go.

November 4th

A very windy day. I saw a large flock of rooks being blown about high in the sky. There were a great number of them and they were being joined by others in two's and three's. They would sweep down towards a field, seemingly to land, then they would swirl up again higher and higher. They appeared to be playing a game. Later I passed a field in which cattle were grazing and there must have been at least a hundred rooks feeding amongst them.

On my way to the river I saw a plant of hogweed still in flower. There were eight long, pale amber flies feeding on it. The heads of the hogweed were being blown to and fro by the strong wind and I don't know how the flies managed to cling on.

As I walked along the path to the main river, a cock pheasant got up with a loud whirring of wings. Immediately birds took off from the surrounding bushes and poplars; a blackbird gave a shrill alarm, thrushes darted away and pigeons soared into the air.

I reached the Itchen, and I saw thirty-seven Canada geese resting and

Ivy leaved duckweed. translucent leaves float on waters surface.

[149]

feeding in one of Mr Gray's fields. It is no wonder he is getting a bit
worried about them for his crop looks very green and lush and the geese
are only too delighted. I was rather worried for I could not see Christmas
Dinner anywhere, although I walked up and down the bank opposite his
favourite resting place.

November 5th
I watched birds bathing in a gutter which was full of water because a
cistern had overflowed. The gutter sloped away from the drain pipe, so
the water was deeper at the gutter end. A blackbird was bathing at the
deep end, a coal tit and a blue tit in the shallow end nearer the pipe. The
scene reminded me of watching my parents' bird bath on a hot day, when
a thrush sat immersed in the centre while the other birds, a nuthatch, a
robin and a great tit, sat behind him on a low branch. The thrush
splashed, preened, then settled low in the water to cool down, ignoring
the queue.

The cottage has just been painted and it looks colourful; white walls,
thin lines of yellow round each window and a yellow front door to match
the rose that grows next to it, which is still in flower.

The painter took down the three swift boxes that we had put up to
help the birds with their problem of finding a nest this year. The boxes

were quite clean inside; they had not even been used for roosting in. They will be put up again and maybe they will be used next year.

November 13th
As I stood on the sleeper bridge by the chestnut tree I counted fourteen coot in a loose group. The young are now the colour of their parents, but are still slightly smaller. There was one young tufted duck with them. A moorhen skated over the water away from me, its feet leaving a wake of splashes as it went.

I sat on the seat by the fishing hut thinking how few birds there were about on this lovely sunny morning. A few minutes later, a grey wagtail flew low up-river and a wren darted into the may bush. Then I saw a kestrel hunting over the water meadow opposite me, facing the west wind, his body curved, head down, and tail fanned out with two feathers missing from the centre of it. With fast wing-beats and a few glides, he started high over a particular piece of ground, then dropped lower until he was only about ten feet up. He hovered there for a while then fell a few feet and glided away into the wind to another site a short way off. Then he would let the wind blow him back to near the first site and start again. I watched him quarter the ground in this way for fifteen minutes and he failed to swoop on anything in that time. Finally he flew off towards the flighting area to try his luck there. It must be very difficult to see a tiny mouse or field vole amongst the tall dying vegetation of the water meadows, for the plants are falling over now. The leaves of the reeds are yellow ochre and the tassels of the flower heads are nearly black. The hemp agrimony has woolly off-white seeds, and the various foliages have turned to different shades of brown and yellow. The osier's branches are orange again. The soft and sombre colours look lovely in the autumn sunlight.

November 14th
The fine dry weather continues. On nearing the river I was struck by how wide it appears without the bankside vegetation. The water is very low and much cut weed is caught up in the shallows.

[151]

Many of the leaves of the trees have fallen. The big horse chestnut by the sleeper bridge is quite devoid of foliage, and a well-formed bush of privet is a mass of black berries, but has hardly a single leaf.

The low level of the water is accentuated by a fly board, which a few weeks ago was floating half submerged, anchored by a cord from the brick bridge on the carrier, with a stone to keep it in place; it now has its tethered end six inches clear of the water. Only the last two feet are submerged.

The fly board was an invention of William Tunn, a famous water-keeper. He observed that all the bactis family of day flies creep under water to lay their eggs. He further observed that many of the eggs were devoured immediately by caddis larvae crawling up from the river bed. The caddis larvae, however, are not strong enough swimmers to reach the underside of the fly board and they are not able to crawl on to its under surface, as it is separate from the brickwork of the bridge. The eggs of the day flies are, therefore, safe from their attentions and their numbers will increase.

November 18th

Today was a day of high south-west winds and fine driving rain, but once I had braved the elements and ventured out I found it quite warm.

The surface of the river was too disturbed to see into its depths. I was curious to see if there was any spawning activity in the shallows. Along the banks were newly-excavated mole hills and along the fringe darted a wren searching for insects, looking like a little mouse as it crept amongst the bankside vegetation.

As I walked further, I saw a grey wagtail fly on to a raft of weed; and an instant later a moorhen took off with a great commotion about a yard away from me.

When I was walking down the right bank of the river towards Easton road bridge, I saw three of the cygnets standing together in shallow water. I wondered where the fourth was, but presently saw him negotiating the 'white water' which flows under the bridge. When the fourth cygnet had come into calmer water and was about ten or fifteen yards from its

[152]

*November, now a beautiful
purple and green.*

fellows, one of the other cygnets swam to meet him. The two birds approached each other very slowly and, when their bills were almost touching, they bent and extended their necks several times in a greeting display. This behaviour was then adopted by the other two cygnets, the whole display lasting two or three minutes.

November 19th

It had been raining all day when I managed to prise my reluctant husband away from elementary carpentry in the kitchen.

Wrapped in jerseys, coats, scarves and woolly hats, we squelched down to the playing field and over the stile; the rain became heavy as dark clouds scudded low across the sky. The vegetation looked indistinct through the driving rain, and we were forced to shelter under a nearby yew. The bullocks grazing in front of us looked matted, and great wet droplets fell from their horns, but it obviously was not cold enough for them to turn their backs on both rain and prevailing wind.

We walked on hurriedly, feeling very damp, crossing the wooden bridge covered with great round patches of lichen to the fallen willow. Today the lichens showed up well in the rain against the dark slippery wood. I also noticed lines of pale green lichen on the thatched roof of the cottage. The willow was dark green and ivy clad; by its side stood the remains of giant docks, bright red-rust in the rain. All the reeds had been completely flattened; the watercress, however, looks in perfect condition for there have been no harsh frosts as yet. Rafts of colourful leaves lie caught amongst the water weeds, flat against the water's surface. They remind me of pages of pressed flowers.

We crossed to the goose-cropped field and walked along the main river. Pat Fox seems to have been a little over-zealous in his cutting of the bankside vegetation, but it may be that he is looking for bank erosion. Dotted along the path were pale fawn fungi with delicate white gills; they were not very large and smelt exactly like horse mushroom.

Three ducks and a few young pheasants flew overhead as we got over the wet and slippery stile. The road was full of puddles and soggy leaves, whilst above us sloes were silhouetted against the sky, with large bright

[153]

droplets forming on each one; the leaves had already fallen. Flies buzzed in the rain attracting my attention to a few ivy flowers. They smell very unpleasant when wet, but the pollen actually tastes sweet.

With relief we finally made it back to our front door. Hiding in the relative shelter of a step was a small, despondent toad, obviously looking for a place to hibernate. We moved it with the aid of rubber gloves to the bottom of the garden where there is a heap of stones and no danger from traffic.

November 20th

It was still raining when we went to bed last night but we awoke to a sunny, frosty morning. I wish I had gone down to the river early and so enjoyed the white scene it must have presented. By the time I did go down, the frost only remained on dead leaves and grass where the sun had not yet shone.

Half way along Church Lane, I met Muff, the large black shaggy 'poodle'. He was delighted to see me and decided to accompany me on my walk. It was good to be walking with a dog again, although inevitably he disturbed creatures before I got up to them.

We went through the flighting ponds past the old caravan, through the meadow where the cattle graze, and on to the sleeper bridge. I was surprised to see how far advanced the buds of the old chestnut tree were. They shone in the sunlight, sticky and quite large.

As I got over the stile I was pleased to see the domestic goose again. He was standing all alone in his favourite spot on the far side of the main river, there were no other geese to be seen anywhere. When Muff and I appeared on the bridge the goose waddled quickly to the river and joined the almost fully-grown young swan, who was once more on his own. This bird, still with soft brown plumage, must be a cob, for he is large and hissed at the goose as it swam near him – which was sad as that goose likes the company of swans when his own kind are away.

The river has taken on the hue of the soft colours of autumn that are reflected in it; the russets, shades of browns and yellows are mixed with patches of blue from the sky.

[154]

*tiny piece of river-
side ivy*

DECEMBER

December 3rd

I walked along the road to Alresford and turned right into the lane that runs past the Rectory. Up the left bank I saw a broad bare band of earth on both sides of the trunk of a tree; something had been sliding there, and a beaten path led up the steep slope amongst the bare bushes to the field above. I was excited at the thought that young badgers might have been playing there. I clambered up the bank over the thick carpet of fallen leaves and found a dug-out home with a corrugated-iron roof!

Amongst the savagely cut-back bushes and trees of the left bank, I saw both old and newly-made rabbit burrows – these also had paths leading from them to the fields at the top. Pheasants peered at me from the young kale in a field on the right, but their heads disappeared as I walked along.

At the end of the grassy lane I turned back. It was teatime and getting dark; the lights were coming on in the village below. Someone was taking his two large dogs for a walk round the field between me and the cricket pitch. As I clambered over the fence by the firmly-locked large iron gate, three pheasants flew out of the tree beside me. They had already gone to roost.

December 7th

The early days of December have been cold but dry. Well protected against the elements, I set out for the river.

I wandered down the right bank of the carrier, disturbing one or two large trout, which departed hastily with a great bow wave as evidence of their bulk and power.

Past the old shepherd's caravan I noticed that Mr Fox had been at work 'tinning' the bank. This operation consists of fixing corrugated-iron sheeting, where the bank has been eroded over the years, and filling in

Early December, the fruit has become rounded and dark red.

The leaves of the Wild Carrot. Daucus
carota.

behind the corrugated iron with mud dredged from the river bed with a mud pan. The mud pan is a bucket fixed on a long pole and it needs great skill to throw the bucket across the river while letting the pole slip through the hands. The bucket is then retrieved filled with mud, which is deposited on the bank behind the sheeting.

This work is necessary here, for the river has, over the years, become progressively wider through bank erosion. This has slowed down the rate of flow, which is now further decreased by water extraction. The result is that silt and mud are no longer carried downstream, as in the more rapidly moving stretches, but settle on to the river bed. The depth of the mud gets deeper year by year, and progressively the deeper layers become devoid of oxygen; in some cases this results in toxic substances being formed. The end result is that in such areas there is no weed growth, and because of this a great reduction of the habitats of many organisms – such as the nymphs of aquatic flies, which depend on oxygen-rich plants for their survival; they also feed upon the algae on the fronds of the plants.

This tinning operation is of vital importance to the fly fisherman, the quality of whose sport depends upon the quantity of fly life which supports the fish.

It is also of interest indirectly to the naturalist. The wet mud by the side of the river is often covered by the tracks of both animals and birds. On this occasion I could see the bold tracks of the moorhen, whose feet are quite large for the size of the bird. And a little distance away I saw the tracks of a stoat. There were, however, no feathers and no other evidence of a kill; so I presume the stoat was on his way to the river for a leisurely drink.

December 13th
The last two days have been wet and stormy. It was quite fine, however, when I reached the riverbank. I was anxious to see if there were any further tracks of birds or animals in the soft mud, where Mr Fox had been working on the bank. There were only tracks of the moorhen however These were confirmed by my disturbing the bird itself further downstream.

[157]

Ilex aquifolium Bacciflava.
Leaves and flowers similar
to common Holly, but fruit is
bright yellow.

Common Holly.
Ilex aquifolium.

Flowers are four petalled, the buds - deep purple and pink, the flowers white
with veins of pink marking the tips of the petals. These clusters of flowers
smell sweet and quite sickly.

Today the river is not only higher but also quite coloured by the heavy rains, which is very unusual for a chalk stream. The current is stronger and is no longer diverted by cut weed and watercress. The watercress has suffered due to recent frost.

Watercress is looked on with favour by river-keepers as it indicates water of great purity and is a good habitat for nymphs and shrimps. It does not spread unduly until late in the season, and quickly dies at the first touch of frost.

December 14th

The river is clearer today but I could see no fish. A little grebe dived at my approach. Further downstream I saw a grey wagtail hunting for insects on a raft of weed.

I was anxious to find a 'slide' made by the otter, which I had been told about by Mr Fox. He is quite certain that the otter lives in the marshy meadow between the two rivers, and enters the river by means of a slide down the bank.

Sure enough, just where Mr Fox had described it to me, there was a smooth track leading into the water. The watercress had been crushed and the slide looked so smooth that I wondered if it was covered with eel slime. (The eel is the favourite food of the otter.) However, this was not the case and the slide was quite dry. I looked for tracks in the soft earth, but unfortunately the cattle had disturbed the area so much that I was not able to find any.

At this time of year many birds collect in flocks. It appears that mature and immature birds remain together until the next mating season. The moorhen is no exception; and the young birds, whose bills are not yet red like their parents', are to be seen with the adult birds.

Mr Fox told me that he had been duck-shooting with a fellow water-keeper and seen in the distance what appeared to be a collection of peewits, whose broad wings gave the impression of a rather laboured flight. When the birds came nearer, both water-keepers were astonished to see a flight of thirteen heron.

For thirteen herons to fly over two water-keepers with guns was rather

[159]

pushing their luck, and it did not do to enquire too closely if thirteen heron were allowed to fly majestically on their way.

December 15th
Last night's heavy rain has half filled the punt which is used in the operation to maintain the banks. This punt has done great service over the years, since being discovered by Mr Fox.

December 20th
The moles have been very active near the river where the yellow flag irises grow. Every yard or so the earth has been thrown up in dark mounds, intermingled with specks of chalk. But I found many large adult moles dead by the river, and also along muddy paths where the cattle wend their way through the tall thistles to the field bordering the Itchen. This may have been due to the almost wild Siamese cat that I see so often stalking silently through the meadows; yet all were left to rot.

Every year when the leaves have dropped from the trees and only a few berries remain, green ivy stands out vividly on at least half of the trees, making fascinating shapes against the skyline. I painted some colourful ivy I found trailing over the ground; this sterile branch I was hoping to contrast with the fruiting branches later on. The flowers were out now, forming pale greenish-yellow clusters towards the tops of each vine. After the flowers will come the fruit, which eventually ripens in the spring; dull black and fleshy with a rank flavour.

Discovered a yellow-berried holly some distances from the river. It was a tree about one hundred years old, and it was not alone; two of its offspring stood by it. The birds obviously avoid these pale suspicious-looking fruits for the tree was still covered with berries. I forgot to try out this theory on William, the parrot, for when the Christmas decorations went up the inviting red berries were immediately stripped off and eaten, much to his delight, and my consternation. I painted an example of both the red and yellow berries.

I wondered if we'd have a white Christmas, and what effect the snow would have on the plant and animal life in the valley.

[160]